Haunted
Massachusetts

D0485751

0 11557 03221 5

Haunted
Massachusetts

Ghosts and Strange Phenomena
of the Bay State

Cheri Revai

Illustrations by Heather Adel Wiggins

STACKPOLE
BOOKS

Copyright © 2005 by Stackpole Books

Published by
STACKPOLE BOOKS
5067 Ritter Road
Mechanicsburg, PA 17055
www.stackpolebooks.com

All rights reserved, including the right to reproduce this book or portions
thereof in any form or by any means, electronic or mechanical, including
photocopying, recording, or by any information storage and retrieval system,
without permission in writing from the publisher. All inquiries should be
addressed to Stackpole Books.

Printed in the United States of America

10 9 8 7 6 5 4 3 2

First Edition

Design by Beth Oberholtzer
Cover design by Caroline Stover

Library of Congress Cataloging-in-Publication Data

Revai, Cheri, 1963–
    Haunted Massachusetts : ghosts and strange phenomena of the Bay
State / Cheri Revai–1st ed.
        p.   cm.
    Includes bibliographical references.
    ISBN 0-8117-3221-5 (pbk.)
    1. Haunted Places–Massachusetts.   2. Ghosts–Massachusetts.   I.
Title.
BF1472.U6R475   2005
133.1'09744–dc22   2004025254

ISBN 978-0-8117-3221-5

Contents

Contents

Introduction

fear *n.* **1. a.** A feeling of agitation and anxiety caused by present or imminent danger. **b.** A state marked by this feeling. **2.** A feeling of disquiet or apprehension. **Syns:** *fear, fright, dread, terror, horror, panic, alarm, dismay, consternation, trepidation.* These nouns all denote the agitation and anxiety caused by the presence or imminence of danger.

—*American Heritage College Dictionary*, 3rd ed.

FEAR. IT'S BEEN AROUND SINCE THE BEGINNING OF MANKIND. NEITHER evolutionists nor creationists could argue that point. Neanderthals certainly feared what they didn't understand, and at least from a Hollywood perspective, that was probably quite a lot. This was a wild, uncivilized world in those days. (Heck, it still is in many ways.) When the cavemen weren't oohing and aahing and pointing out the wonders around them, they were grunting and groaning about the horrors they encountered.

Adam and Eve understood the concept of fear the moment they disobeyed God and suffered the consequences—immediate expulsion from their impossibly safe haven, the Garden of Eden. Suddenly they were cast ill prepared into the "real world," having no clue as to what dangers were ahead or what evil lurked behind in the shadows. They were completely alone in a strange, new world, and the unknown must indeed have been very frightening to them.

Fast-forward to the first Native Americans carving their way through the primitive land that would be called Massachusetts. Their early experiences of inexplicable phenomena spawned a myriad of legends and folktales for future generations to ponder. They saw colossal faces on mountainsides, butterflies escorting departing souls to the Great Spirit beyond, vindictive phantoms rowing swiftly across pristine lakes to settle old scores, and more. Much more. But if they could invent stories to explain the seemingly supernatural events that inspired both awe and fear in their people—explain it as only they could, with a combination of fact, fantasy, and pure conjecture—then the unknown would make sense. And when something makes sense, it can be accepted and dealt with *fearlessly*. It was a brilliant coping mechanism. And thanks to the resultant legends, the early history of our land is painted with, as they say, "all the colors of the wind."

Like Adam and Eve and the Native Americans before them, the first Pilgrims to arrive on Massachusetts' shores boldly forged ahead into a strange, new world (to them, anyway). Out of necessity, they faced hostilities and obstacles head-on, but this unfamiliar land held much for them to fear. They found hideous creatures, and dreadful diseases befell their people. Bloodthirsty pirates and sea monsters lurked just offshore, and ghosts and demons lay around practically every corner, it seemed. But worst of all, were the witches. Perhaps these were the most misunderstood—and therefore the most feared—of all beings. Before long, diseases weren't the only epidemics. There was an epidemic of fear—a mass hysteria of never-before-seen proportions. It was fear of the unknown; fear of . . . the witches. Paranoia set in. The majority of people under Puritan rule believed that witches wielded horrific powers bestowed on them by Satan himself. What to do, what to do? They had to be eliminated, of course—and in most unpleasant ways. So the regrettable time of the Salem witch trials began, and yet more unfortunate victims were added to the increasingly volatile pot of restless souls in the newly settled land. "Double, double, toil and trouble; fire burn and cauldron bubble . . ."

The course of the next several centuries set Massachusetts up to become what is likely the most spirit-laden region in the entire country. The state saw maritime disasters, wars, massacres, intentional flooding of entire townships, the shameless disruption of ancient burial grounds, mining disasters, and countless other calamities—often in the name of progress. If the so-called witches of Salem had been responsible (which they weren't), they could not have cast a finer spell to summon the dead. Today the Bay State is teeming with spirits.

For an author of my particular genre—regional ghost stories—Massachusetts is a dream. This book was truly a pleasure to write. I found hundreds of stories to research and consider, and yet I barely scratched the surface. Here I offer you a humble smattering of the endless stories of hauntings and strange phenomena that have taken place in Massachusetts in the past several hundred years or more. Many of these stories are still ongoing, and some, I dare say, may not even have reached their climax yet. Many others have been resurrected here to ensure their survival.

Native Bay Staters may wonder why this book does not include some places that "everyone knows" are haunted. The answer is simple: There just wasn't enough room—not for merely one volume of *Haunted Massachusetts*. But I hope this book whets the reader's appetite for more. I think it will.

Western Massachusetts

WESTERN MASSACHUSETTS CONSISTS OF FRANKLIN COUNTY, THE Berkshires, and the greater Springfield area. It's a vast land of primeval forests, isolated hill towns, farmlands that seem locked in turn-of-the-century time, and ancient routes such as the Mohawk Trail, which traverses Franklin County and the Berkshires. Urban areas of culture, entertainment, and family adventure dot the landscape, but it's the simple, unhurried atmosphere permeating the rest of this region that makes it one of New England's favorite vacation spots for those hoping to get away from the hustle and bustle of metropolitan life. While the charming inns, traditional roadside diners, and old-fashioned country stores certainly are nostalgia-inducing, nothing makes the past seem more palpable than, say, a genuine ghost train from the past—or a covered bridge haunted by a woman murdered in 1704. Suffice it to say, thar's ghosts in them thar hills, and I intend to tell you about them!

The Bloody Pit

The five-mile-long railroad tunnel through Hoosac Mountain near North Adams has been called many things, including the Bloody Pit and the Tunnel from Hell, but its proper name is Hoosac Tunnel. It was built in the 1850s through the 1870s to provide a direct rail route between Boston and Troy, New York. As with many early engineering feats of this magnitude, countless lives were lost during construction—and some estimates put the number on the Hoosac Tunnel project as high as two hundred.

Two of the tunnel's victims died during an explosion when a man named Ringo Kelley detonated the blast prematurely—before the pair had made it to a safe spot. Kelley, though not officially accused of any crime, disappeared shortly after a hearing on the disaster and wasn't seen for a full year. This, of course, caused even more speculation about the role he must have played in the tragedy. Had he skipped town, afraid of being found out? To this day, nobody knows where he went that year, but on the anniversary of the tragedy the following year, his body was found strangled to death in a hole in the tunnel—right in the very spot where the two victims had lost their lives, presumably because of his careless handling of the explosives. Kelley's murderer was never found. Some say it was probably an angry relative of one of the victims, but others believe it was the vengeful ghosts of the two men. The slaying marked the beginning of paranormal incidents inside the tunnel.

After Kelley's body was found, many laborers refused to return to work in the tunnel, fearing that it was cursed, not to mention haunted by bitter ghosts. So many men reported hearing disembodied voices crying out in agony that work on the tunnel nearly came to a screeching halt, prompting railroad officials to call in two investigators to quash the men's fears. It didn't help matters when the investigators heard the moans, too. They finally concluded that it wasn't the wind—yet they hesitated to say what else it might have been.

After another deadly explosion in 1873 took the lives of an unlucky thirteen laborers, area citizens admitted to hearing cries near the pit, and laborers reported seeing phantom workers carrying shovels toward the work site, but leaving no footsteps in the snow. The apparitions ceased after the last body from the explosion was finally removed from the tunnel. At other times, people have heard cries and groans coming from deep within the mountain, and unexplained voices whispering excitedly. Ghost lanterns have been seen moving along the tunnel, as if being carried by human hands, when in actuality, nobody was there to carry them. Apparitions have been reported—several especially memorable ones being headless. One man reported being manhandled to the point of unconsciousness by someone he never saw after he was lured into the tunnel by "strange voices." Another man fled from the tunnel in terror and was never seen again, though his team of horses was found in the woods nearby.

No wonder Hoosac Tunnel is said to be one of New England's most haunted places. But the property is owned by Conrail and is clearly posted, meaning *no trespassing.* The laborers who walked off the job during construction of the tunnel were on the right track, so to speak. They firmly believed the cursed tunnel was best left alone. Consider it off-limits, just as the Indians did when they called the mountain through which it goes Hoosac, meaning "forbidden" in the Mohawk language.

The Legend of Bash-Bish Falls

Long before white man settled on the Atlantic coast of America, a beautiful Mohican woman named Bash-Bish was accused of adultery and sentenced to death by drowning, despite her claims of innocence. Bash-Bish was tied to a canoe, to be released at the top of Massachusetts' highest waterfall in the town of Alandar on Mount Washington, where she would presumably plunge to her death below.

The Indians, including Bash-Bish's infant daughter, White Swan, gathered sadly at the appointed hour, but seconds before they commenced their grim task, a fine, sunlit mist formed and surrounded the accused woman. At the same moment, a ring of dazzling butterflies encircled her head. Was it a message from the Great Spirit, or the work of a demon? While the other Mohicans stood transfixed by the scene, Bash-Bish took the opportunity to break away, running to the edge of the falls and leaping bravely over into the pool of water below, thus sealing her own fate. The mystical butterflies spiraled gracefully down behind her. Her body disappeared into the water below the falls and was never recovered. The Indians, rather than believe they had witnessed a divine intervention, thought that only a witch would avoid punishment using the black magic Bash-Bish had surely employed. Nonetheless, they embraced her innocent baby as one of the tribe, raising White Swan to adulthood.

Years later, White Swan, now a lovely young woman, was distraught over not being able to bear a child for her husband, the

tribal chief's son. Though her husband was kind and loving, and their marriage was solid, he was required by tradition to take a second wife who would give him an heir. Devastated, White Swan journeyed to the top of Bash-Bish Falls daily, desperately seeking solace from her mother's spirit. Her husband tried to comfort her as best he could, bringing her various gifts from nature, but her despondency grew. One night, White Swan had a dream. In it was Bash-Bish, seeking a reunion with her only child. She told her daughter to join her, and because White Swan had been taught by her people that dreams should be regarded as prophecy, she took it very seriously and awaited further direction from the spirit.

One night at dusk, just as White Swan's husband approached her at the top of the falls with his latest gift—a rare, white butterfly—she heard her mother's ethereal voice saying, "It is time, White Swan." The young woman never saw the look of horror on her husband's face as she leaped over the falls, so mesmerized was she by the voice of her mother. Her husband dropped the butterfly and grabbed for White Swan, but he wasn't quick enough. She was gone, and the white butterfly fluttered down the eighty-foot falls behind her. He plunged after her, hoping to somehow save her, but his selfless act led to his own death. His body was found in the pool beneath the falls the next day. White Swan's body, like her mother's, was never recovered.

Some say that the soft, unearthly voices of women have been heard near the falls in Bash-Bish State Forest, perhaps Bash-Bish trying to summon another wounded soul to join her beneath the falls. Several people have seen the falling water take on the shape of a woman, believed to be Bash-Bish or White Swan, and still others have seen a smiling female face as they looked down into the crystalline pool of water below the falls.

The Phantom Canoe of Pontoosuc Lake

Pontoosuc Lake in Pittsfield is often referred to as "the crown jewel of the Berkshires" for its breathtaking beauty and serenity. But many years ago, it was called the Shon-keek-moon-keek by the Mohegan Indians. It's hard to imagine the tragic event that tainted its pristine image and created the poignant reasoning behind its original namesake.

Moon-keek was an Indian maiden whose father was the chief. The chief's brother had a son named Shon-keek. Moon-keek and Shon-keek grew up together and eventually realized that their love went far beyond that of first cousins. They wished to wed, but their tribe believed that misfortune came upon tribes that permitted the marrying of cousins. Undeterred, the young lovers came up with a plan that would permit their union. They would meet on the island in Pontoosuc Lake and travel to a tribe in the northeast that would be more agreeable to their living together as husband and wife. They decided that if someone tried to stop them, they would meet beneath the lake, in spirit, rather than continue to live apart.

The anticipated evening arrived, and Moon-keek rowed hastily to the island, eager to get on with the plan. Through the darkness, she could see the approach of Shon-keek's canoe, but then her happy heart skipped a beat. She saw Shon-keek slump and begin to lean overboard. Just beyond his canoe, Moon-keek spotted Nock-awando—the jealous man she had spurned—rowing fast and furious, with a murderous glint in his eye. The bow that had sent the deadly arrow through her beloved Shon-keek's heart was at Nock-awando's side. In an instant, Moon-keek pushed off from shore toward Shon-keek's canoe, hoping desperately to catch him before he went under. Just as she reached for him, down he went, and she followed him deliberately, as they had agreed. When the bodies of the two came to rest on the floor of the lake, their spirits resumed their mission in the two empty canoes. Nockawando was unaware of what had transpired. He had seen Moon-keek rowing gallantly toward the fatally wounded Shon-keek in the moonlight, but he never saw her go overboard. He didn't know she was dead. All he had seen was her likeness stopping briefly at Shon-keek's canoe before continuing on toward his own canoe. But as she approached, Nockawando realized that he could see right through her eyes as she glared at him contemptuously. Then he watched in horror as both canoes rowed silently away, side by side, into the heavy mist that was settling over the lake.

He returned to his camp a raving maniac—for the ordeal had made him insane—and he admitted his guilt to the tribe, as if it would appease the two angry spirits and keep them from haunting him more than they already were. The Indians searched in vain for the bodies of the drowned couple. Though they were never recovered, the lovers apparently are together in spirit, as they had desired. Their apparitions, depicted in the following poem, have been seen paddling across the lake, eternally trying to reach the Other Side.

> But oft from the Indian hunter's camp
> This lover and maid so true
> Are seen, the hour of midnight damp,
> To cross the lake by a firefly lamp,
> And paddle their white canoe.

Bigfoot in Berkshire County

Bigfoot sightings are more common in the northeastern United States than you might have realized. The Bigfoot Field Researchers Organization (BFRO) lists two interesting cases from Berkshire County that share similar characteristics, even though they happened more than a hundred years apart.

An October 18, 1879, article in the *New York Times* described an apparent Bigfoot sighting on the Vermont-Massachusetts border:

> Much excitement prevails among the sportsmen in this vicinity over the story that a wild man was seen on Friday by two young men while hunting in the mountains south of Williamstown. The young men describe the creature as being about five feet high, resembling a man in form and movement, but covered all over with bright red hair, and having a long straggling beard, and with very wild eyes. When first seen, the creature sprang from behind a rocky cliff and started for the woods nearby. When mistaking it for a bear or other wild animal, one of the men fired, and, it is thought, wounded it, for with fierce cries of pain and rage, it turned on its assailants, driving them before it at high speed. They lost their guns and ammunition in their flight and dared not return for fear of encountering the strange being.

BFRO Report #1199 describes a much more recent Bigfoot sighting by a lone individual hiking in the October Mountain State Forest in Lenoxdale in July 1989. The sighting occurred on a well-established trail near the top of October Mountain. The witness said he spotted a far-off creature that he at first believed to be a common black bear. When he used his binoculars to get a better look, he realized that it was a very tall animal with reddish hair. It was slightly stooped, and its body and head were massive. The elongated face had less hair on it than the head, and it seemed to have no neck, but it looked more human than animal. The hiker could see it grubbing for food and stacking stones neatly in a pile by its side. In a moment of either great courage or great stupidity (the line between the two is often very fine), he decided to move in for a closer look. He couldn't believe what he was seeing and wanted to be sure it wasn't some kind of a hoax.

It was then that he realized the arms of the beast went down past its knees, and its hands—though human in shape—were unusually large. The creature lumbered slowly back into the forest at about the same moment that the hiker had expended his last ounce of courage and made haste for the trail. It's no wonder Bigfoot has eluded captivity for so long. He scares off anyone who gets too close!

The Phantom Express

Ghost trains are not an unusual phenomenon. Since the first steam engine was invented, people all over the world have reported seeing or hearing mysterious locomotives that appear out of the blue and quickly vanish into thin air. Sometimes only the rumble of the approaching steam engine is heard and felt; other times, nothing is seen but the headlights coming down the track—unattached to any actual train.

Pittsfield once had a phantom train, according to author Joseph Citro in *Passing Strange*. Several eyewitnesses saw it on two separate occasions in 1958, while dining at a local restaurant. Both times the train was barreling toward Boston, and it looked so real that stunned observers could even see the coals that fueled the engine. Railway officials were deluged with queries about the strange sightings and quickly conducted an investigation to determine who was guilty of the unauthorized use of their tracks. Their search was fruitless. No train, let alone an outdated *steam* engine like the one described by the witnesses, had even been on that particular track at the time of the sightings. It was as if a glimpse of the past had somehow broken through the space-time barrier for a few fleeting, unforgettable moments.

Maybe the ghost train was Housatonic Railroad's doomed passenger train of 1865. This train was en route to Pittsfield from Bridgeport, Connecticut, when the conductor was forced to back it up because another train on the single-lane track was disabled and blocking its way. As the ill-fated train was backing up, it collided with yet another locomotive making an unscheduled maiden voyage from the same station. Eleven passengers died that day, and twenty-seven were injured. Maybe, nearly a hundred years after its tragic collision, the phantom train finally made it to Pittsfield.

The ghost train of Pittsfield is not to be confused with the legendary "Ghost Train" of 1890s fame. The popular White Train, as it was officially called, was owned by New York & New England Railroad and actually had nothing to do with ghosts at all, except that it was as white as one. Even the crew dressed immaculately, all decked out in white. This dazzling luxury train ran from Boston to New York City in the late nineteenth century but was discontinued when it became too difficult to maintain its cleanliness. It was a remarkable sight while it lasted, though, as was the so-called "phantom express" of Pittsfield.

Haunted Houghton Mansion

John Widders loved Mary Houghton, the youngest daughter of North Adams's first mayor, Albert C. Houghton. Widders worked as a chauffeur for the Houghton family for many years in the late 1800s and early 1900s. He was somewhat of a surrogate uncle to the Houghton children, for the three girls adored him, and the feeling was certainly mutual. But he had a particular soft spot for Mary, whom he'd watched grow from infancy to womanhood.

One regrettable summer day in August 1911, the Houghtons set out for Vermont for dinner, with Widders at the wheel. It was a good day for a leisurely outing—who could work when it was so balmy, anyway? Family friend Sybil Hutton went along for the ride, and for a while, everyone was enjoying a pleasant drive. But just as Mrs. Houghton had feared, the steep and perilous Pownal Center Hill, which they would have to go over, was still under construction. It was no secret that she hated that hill—and with good reason, she would soon learn. At the top of the hill, Widders was forced to go far out and around a team of horses that was hogging the road. Suddenly the gravel shoulder of the road collapsed, sending the Houghton vehicle careening down the slope with an avalanche of dust and dirt behind it. Sybil Hutton and Mary Houghton—the love of Widders's life—died in the accident. John blamed himself. Without Mary, he didn't want to go on. Overcome by grief and guilt, he felt that his only option was to join her. Widders went to the horse barn behind the family mansion and shot himself in the head the morning after the accident. Tragedy followed tragedy, and three years later, A. C. Houghton died from a stroke.

The Lafayette-Greylock Masonic Lodge purchased the Houghton Mansion on Church Street in 1920. According to Nicholas Mantello, the president of the Masonic association that maintains and uses the building, he and the brethren have felt the presence of an unsettled spirit in the lodge ever since—so often that Mantello now calls upstairs to the ghost, "Good morning (or good evening), Mr. Widders!" whenever he enters or leaves the building. More than one person has felt an icy chill go through or past them, and phantom footsteps, not to mention slams, bangs, and creaks, have been heard by many. Mostly, the footsteps sound as if they are tediously climbing the inexplicably drafty stairs to the third-floor servant quarters where John Widders slept, prompting many to speculate that the heartbroken man still hasn't forgiven himself and found peace. Even though he joined the Houghtons in the family burial plot, he has yet to join them in the afterlife.

Mantello related a story to me about a telemarketer who was hired a few years ago to raise money for the organization. "The man in charge told me that every evening after eleven or so [while he worked late in the lodge tallying each day's totals], he would get chills up his spine and get the feeling of Mr. Widders's presence. One evening, the feeling of a presence was so overwhelming that he left the lodge, leaving the lights on and the door unlocked. What made the story so comical is that the man stood six feet, five inches tall and was a good three hundred twenty pounds. He was a big man with a southern drawl and a booming voice. When he told the story, you just had to picture it in your mind—this man of large stature running down the stairs and out the door. Priceless."

As I was writing this story, Mantello had yet another run-in with

Widders's ghost. The lodge had an evening event called Neighborhood Night Out. When Mantello got to the lodge the night of that event, he was telling the brethren about the draft I had shown him of this story, and two young men and a young lady overheard him. They had never heard about the Widders tragedy or the ghost, and they asked if they could have a tour. Mantello agreed, and when only he and the youths were left in the building, he started telling them the story. It was thundering and lightning as they followed him through the building, listening wide-eyed to the details of the accident and suicide. "As we were moving to the stairs to go to the third floor where Mr. Widders had his quarters, a noise like a pipe being scraped shot through the hall," Mantello told me. "We all stopped in our tracks like a choreographed dance. I turned to see the three of them with gaping mouths, where smiles were only moments before." They all bravely agreed to continue with the tour nonetheless. When they reached Widders's room, Mantello said, "The thunder was coming almost simultaneously with the flashes of lightning. I felt very uneasy, like I was intruding, and suggested that we move on quickly. We did continue to explore the third floor, but the noises, bangs, and thumps not associated with the storm continued to intensify, becoming louder and more frequent. It was definitely time to get out!"

The young trio hurried down the stairs, with Mantello trailing behind, turning off light switches. He asked them, "Well, do you believe in Widders now?" Unanimously, they answered with a resounding yes. It was a night they surely would never forget. Mantello himself was a bit surprised at the intensity of paranormal clattering that seemed so perfectly well coordinated with his tour. He saw his captive audience to the front door, turned off the porch light, and checked the lock, then turned around with a grin on his face and a shake of his head and called out to his ghostly accomplice, "Good night, Mr. Widders!" And good show!

Eunice Williams's Restless Spirit

On February 29, 1704, Eunice Williams had just given birth to a healthy baby boy. She was still basking in the glow of having brought a new life into the world when a band of passing French and Indians attacked the village of Deerfield, where she and her husband, the Reverend John Williams, lived with their children. Many citizens were killed right then and there—including the newborn Williams child, who was ripped out of his mother's arms and killed while the helpless and horrified parents watched. About a hundred Deerfield citizens were then herded up and taken captive. These included John and Eunice, as well as their three remaining children, all girls. They were driven in a freezing, brutal march toward Canada, and anyone not able to keep up was immediately struck down and left to die.

Eunice knew she would never make it. Her body was still traumatized by childbirth just hours earlier. As her energy waned, she whispered good-bye to her husband and prayed that he and the children would somehow survive the ordeal. Then she fell back while crossing a frigid river in Greenfield and was instantly hacked to death by the blow of a tomahawk. Her bloodied body drifted away with the current as the marchers—each mourning for their individual losses—were forced to continue on without pause. For two years, John Williams and his three daughters were held captive in Canada. When they were finally set free, one of the children—the young Eunice, named after her mother—refused to leave. She preferred to marry an Indian and, in so doing, turned her back on her English heritage, becoming one of the savages who had murdered her mother in cold blood.

This had to be more than Eunice's poor spirit could handle. It was horrible enough having her newborn child torn away from her and then being killed herself, but to have her own flesh and blood disregard those same things was unfathomable. Many people believe Eunice's restless spirit still haunts the river and nearby covered bridge that was later named after her. Her ghost has been seen both in the water and inside the bridge, reportedly responding to motorists who stop their engines, turn off their headlights, and honk once.

The Face on the Mountain

Ghosts can do some pretty impressive things, but nothing compares to the giant face carved into the side of a mountain by the man for whom that mountain was named. How else can the coincidental likeness be explained?

Chief Greylock of the Waronoke tribe (and later the Missisquoi tribe) lived in a secret cave on the side of Mount Greylock in the late 1600s. He made his living by hunting, trapping animals for fur, and trading with the British, until the wild game dwindled because of the increase in local human population. So Greylock moved several times, finally settling at Missisquoi Bay, where he built "Greylock's Castle." His tribe took in many refugees from the wars, but they were forced to choose sides when war broke out between the French and the British. Greylock and his warriors aligned themselves with the French, and the chief became famous for his success in leading raids against the British well into his sixties. Though many British governors ordered his arrest, Greylock eluded capture and was never defeated. Berkshire County will never forget him, and how could they? His face now appears on the side of Mount Greylock.

In 1901, a landslide on the mountain left a path called the Chief's Steps on the eastern slope. Then in May 1990, a heavy rainfall that lasted for four days caused another landslide, leaving in its wake the giant stone face of Greylock, which now watches over the land the old chief once valiantly fought to preserve for his tribe.

Central
Massachusetts

CENTRAL MASSACHUSETTS IS SYNONYMOUS WITH WORCESTER COUNTY.
Here in the heart of the state is where America's industrial revolution was said to have begun. Two prominent locations in the region are the city of Worcester, the second-largest city in the state, and a massive watershed known as the Quabbin Reservoir, a repository of inexplicable phenomena. The mysterious Quabbin Reservoir is located partially in Western Massachusetts' Pioneer Valley, but mostly it lies within Worcester County. The Central Massachusetts region boasts of haunted Quaker cemeteries, underwater ghost towns, strange atmospheric anomalies, alien encounters, demonic possessions, haunted mills, and the famous legend of Lucy Keyes. If you've never heard of her, you will . . .

The Legend of Lucy Keyes

In 1751, the Keyes family was the fourth family to settle in Princeton. When Robert and Martha Keyes moved to the foothills on the southeastern slope of Wachusett Mountain, they felt truly blessed. They had purchased two hundred acres of virgin forest and set about clearing their densely wooded land and building a modest homestead. There was much work to be done, and every member

of the young family chipped in—except Lucy. Lucy was their beautiful, blue-eyed baby and was doted on accordingly.

On April 14, 1755, Martha sent her two older girls, Patty, age seven, and Anna, nine, to fetch some white sand from the shore of Wachusett Lake to sprinkle on the wooden floor of their home as a scouring agent. The girls knew their way there, having traveled the tree-marked path many times before. But four-year-old Lucy was told to stay behind by her protective mother. She was too small to keep up with her sisters, and Martha enjoyed her company. Martha sat back down at her spinning wheel, just several feet from where Lucy was contentedly playing near the front door outside. Shortly after, when the family returned home from their individual tasks, Martha noticed that Lucy wasn't around. They split up and searched everywhere, yelling loudly to Lucy, hoping that she had just fallen asleep somewhere and would hear them. But it soon became apparent that Lucy was missing. She must have tried to follow her sisters through the woods and gotten lost. Search teams were set up from Princeton and surrounding communities. Even the miserable old hermit Tilly Littlejohn, who lived adjacent to the Keyes, joined in on the search. Martha, who was devastated beyond words, spent hours calling her young daughter's name—"Lucy, Lucy!"—and her voice carried over the hills, where it was heard by many as a sad reminder of the family's plight.

Eventually the search parties gave up, when everyone agreed that there was no hope for Lucy to have survived more than a week without food or shelter. Her only chance of being alive was if she'd been captured by Indians, and that was a strong theory at one point, thanks to their hermit neighbor, who told the searchers he'd seen a band of wild Mohawks in the same woods the day before. It was common in those days for women and children to be taken captive by Indians in the unsettled territory. Robert Keyes and several other gentlemen followed up on leads to Indian camps in Massachusetts and other northeastern states where they were told young white girls were being held captive. Each visit proved fruitless. Lucy's father spent the rest of his life going from Indian camp to Indian camp, hoping to find his lost daughter, but to no avail. In the meantime, Martha—pushed to the brink of insanity by her sorrow—continued faithfully calling to Lucy every single night for the rest of her life . . . and even after her death. Thirty-one years after Lucy's disappearance, Martha passed away, never knowing what had become of her daughter. That must be why her distraught calls continue to be heard sometimes at dusk. Various people have reported a woman's disembodied voice calling out "Luuu-cy!" near the Keyes property over the years since the tragedy.

The truth about what happened to Lucy Keyes was never revealed until August 12, 1815—long after Robert and Martha Keyes had passed on. On that date, a letter of confession was submitted to the postmaster of Westminster, as dictated by none other than Tilly Littlejohn, the hermit neighbor of the Keyes. After years of being haunted by his crime, Tilly decided to clear his conscience on his deathbed, so he had his housekeeper write out his confession. He had come across Lucy on the path leading to the lake on the day she went missing, and he was immediately overcome with hatred for her father, with whom he'd had a land disagreement. [He and Robert Keyes had gone to court, and Keyes was awarded a chunk of land that Tilly believed was his.] When the little girl looked up at him with fear in her eyes, he grew even angrier, because that was how he perceived all children looked at him. He hated children. He hated that look. The fact that Robert Keyes had a wife and three children and all that prime property, and Tilly himself had nothing by comparison, was a smoldering bone of contention. For that one instant in the woods with the small girl who looked up at him with her father's eyes, he became too upset to even think straight. In an insane fit of blind rage that he would regret for the rest of his life, he smacked the child on the side of the head, knocking her unconscious. Realizing immediately that he'd made a huge mistake and couldn't allow her to live or be found, because she would give him away, he dealt two more blows—this time fatal—to her tiny head with a heavy stone. Then he stuffed her little body into a rotted-out log and played along with the search parties, until he realized they were being so thorough that he'd have to hide her in a better place. So he buried her in the hole left by the roots of a large fallen tree and covered her body with brush and leaves.

Soon the mournful calling by Martha each night was more than Tilly could take, so he moved to the Mohawk River in New York State, where he again became a hermit until his death in his nineties. Unfortunately for him, simply moving away wasn't enough to stop the sounds and visions that haunted his sleep. He still could see the small child's shocked face when he dealt the first blow—he saw it practically every night in his dreams—and Martha's sorrowful voice reverberated in his mind endlessly. His only escape would be death, and he welcomed it when it finally came after such an unbearably long life.

Many people believe that both mother and child still haunt the mountainside, each looking for the other. A woman's sorrowful voice is carried on the wind of Wachusett Mountain, and a small child's fresh footprints are seen in the snow on top of the mountain by employees of the ski resort—at two in the morning. The legend has become so famous that a movie is in the works called "The Legend of Lucy Keyes," by native Princeton producer and writer John Stimpson. You can be sure you'll be hearing more about what Stimpson calls "the lost child of Wachusett Mountain" in the very near future.

Spider Gates

Friends Cemetery or Quaker Cemetery are the proper, if mundane, names of what is commonly known as Spider Gates in Leicester, so called because of the sunburst designs that vaguely resemble mutant spiders or their wavy webs on the main entrance gates. What's so unusual about this modest little graveyard nestled in the woods of Leicester? Lots—if you believe the local legends.

For one thing, it's reputedly haunted. People have heard strange voices and otherworldly screams emanating from within the four stone walls that border the property. Many claim to be overcome with eerie sensations when passing through the entrance gates— even nonarachnophobiacs! The area is said to be unusually quiet, with none of the expected nature sounds, such as birds chirping, but the Worcester airport borders the property, and that may have more to do with the lack of wildlife than anything supernatural. But then there are the legends . . .

Allegedly, the property has been the site of devil worship, gateways to hell, strange disappearances, a vanishing graveyard, unexplained sounds, cult activities, and more. Because of the wildfirelike spread of such rumors, the cemetery is now heavily patrolled by the local police department, and in order to visit it, one must obtain permission from the private owners, the Worcester–Pleasant Street Friends Meeting. A specific code of conduct is required at all times while on the property. This is, after all, sacred ground, and it should be treated respectfully.

If the raised, twenty-foot area of the graveyard sometimes called "the altar" ever *was* used by devil worshipers, as has been reported, it no longer is or should be. Satanism is strictly prohibited at Spider Gates, contrary to rumors that say otherwise. The raised area is actually the foundation to where the old Friends Meeting House once stood.

At least three people are rumored to have died in the cemetery—two of them from a tree now called "the hanging tree." In the 1930s, the story goes, a man left his girlfriend in his car when it broke down near the main entrance of the cemetery while he ran for help. He never returned, and the legend says that a policeman later found his body dangling from a tree in the cemetery. Fifty-some years later, a distraught teenager supposedly hanged himself from the same tree; some say he was instructed to do so by sinister forces within the cemetery. Neither hanging was ever reported in the media, so, like most legends, the stories are unsubstantiated. The third legend is that a young lady intended to stay in a cave she'd found on the property to get away from her feuding family, and her mutilated body was later found in the nearby woods. No report was ever filed, however, and the body, if there was one, was never officially identified. But the legend has it that the woman's cigarette packs were found in the cave she had planned to stay in. Whether there's an ounce of truth to any of these stories is not for general public knowledge.

Some of the phenomena believed to be possible at the cemetery are purely speculative. A portal to another dimension has been said to be accessible to those who walk alongside three of the surrounding stone walls in a particular sequence. As of yet, nobody has accomplished that seemingly simple task. Then there are the seven alleged gateways leading to the "river of the dead" that can be found between the graveyard and the brook (which is the symbolic river). No actual gates exist, however, and if anybody ever found their way through the *unseen* gates, they never returned to tell about it. (Why would anyone want to find that river, anyway?)

One of the more interesting stories associated with Spider Gates is an elusive graveyard in the nearby woods that a person can see only once. Nobody has ever located it a second time, and nobody has ever actually entered it. But many have reported seeing a mysterious graveyard through the woods or over the brook, and when they look again, it's gone, or when they approach, they find that it's not where it had been. As in *Alice in Wonderland,* in Spider Gates cemetery, nothing is as it seems.

The Strange Mr. Snow

Asa Snow was an eccentric man. In 1840, he moved into a farmhouse at the crossroads between Dana and Petersham, where he remained until his death thirty-two years later. According to those who knew of him, he was as strange in life as he was in death. Snow's nickname was Popcorn, because he subsisted primarily on popcorn and milk—pretty humble provisions for a man who presumably made a small fortune loan-sharking.

In August 1844, Snow's first wife committed suicide by hanging herself with a strip of cloth from the dress she was wearing, and many locals blamed Snow for making the poor woman insane by his eccentric behavior. Snow buried her lovingly in an old cemetery across the brook from his house, and the following year, he had the sad task of burying his young daughter next to her. But their remains were disinterred in 1868, when Snow had them moved to an elaborate family tomb he'd built in the same graveyard. Besides constructing the large tomb, Snow became obsessed with every last detail of his own eventual burial. He had a coffin maker build a strong metal casket for him with a ten-inch glass window at the head end. This was not so his spirit could look out; it was so a hired undertaker could look *in* on him for seven days after his death, just to make sure he truly was dead.

When death finally came, it did so with an ironic twist. Snow was a vegetarian, but he died of heart failure while lugging a heavy pig carcass for others to enjoy up the front steps of his house on Thanksgiving Day 1872. Snow's second wife, perhaps wanting to be certain her impossible-to-live-with husband wasn't coming back, told the undertaker Snow had hired that three days was quite long enough to check on her husband's casket, short-changing Snow of four of the days he had been promised by the undertaker.

It didn't take long for curiosity seekers to break into the tomb to see if the rumors about the man with a window in his casket and popcorn as his cushion were true. For forty years, Snow's remains had stayed intact. In fact, the condition of his body was remarkably unchanged, no doubt thrilling the many brave onlookers who ventured into the tomb, but also creating even more rumors regarding the man named Popcorn. This time, the rumors were not about his strange life, but about his strange spirit.

One tale was that Snow's ghost left the tomb every November 15 (there's no explanation for that date) to visit his wife's grave nearby. Another was about a man from Boston who was dared to visit the tomb on that night and leave a jug of whiskey on top of Snow's casket as proof he had been there. The man accepted the challenge for $10, tied his horse outside of the tomb, and went in. Shortly after entering, he heard his horse go berserk. He hustled outside, but the horse was already a mile down the road, obviously traumatized. The next day, when the shaken man brought his challenger to the tomb to prove he had been there, the bottle of whiskey he had left there was smashed to pieces. This left no doubt in either man's mind that Snow had indeed haunted the area the previous night, just as the legend said.

With all of the tales going around, it was just a matter of time before some disrespectful trespasser smashed in the glass on Snow's casket, and after this, decay set in rapidly. Town of Petersham officials had the tomb immediately sealed back up securely, but in 1944, it was once again disturbed. The Metropolitan Water Commission relocated all of the graves in that cemetery to the Quabbin Park Cemetery in Ware before flooding four towns, including Dana, to create the massive Quabbin Reservoir. Not only was the tomb that Snow had put so much thought into destroyed in the move, but his home was leveled, as were those of everyone in the four lost communities. There had to be a lot of unhappy campers—both living and dead—as a result, none the least of whom was Popcorn Snow.

The Q-Files of Quabbin Reservoir

In 1939, the Swift River Valley was flooded by the Metropolitan Water Commission to create the Quabbin Reservoir, which would provide fresh water to the Boston area, a hundred miles to the west. The mountaintops became islands in a few years' time. As you can imagine, the residents of the towns and villages that were displaced were not happy. Forced out of their homes, they were offered measly compensation for their losses and required to relocate. Houses, churches, and businesses were leveled. Graves were dug up and transferred to the new Quabbin Park Cemetery, built specifically for the dead from the four "lost towns" of Dana, Enfield, Greenwich, and Prescott. The only graveyards left untouched were those known to be old Native American burial grounds. For some reason, the decision makers chose not to disturb the dead from such consecrated locations. Did they think it might upset Native American spirits but not those of their white brothers? They thought wrong. Even though the Indian burial grounds were undisturbed, a whole lot of other equally sacred grounds of non-natives were violated—and now Quabbin Reservoir is a paranormal hot spot that some equate to an enormous spirit portal, a doorway to another dimension.

Plenty of ghost stories originate from the two-hundred-square-mile watershed encompassing the reservoir, including the tale of Popcorn Snow and numerous reports of "ghost lights" behaving erratically near or on the water. But other inexplicable things have been seen as well. So many, in fact, that the reservoir could easily keep a catalog of its oddities and call it the Q-Files. Large crocodiles were sighted in 1922, and smaller crocs were actually captured more recently. Reports of cougars or giant cats, which are supposedly extinct in the Bay State, number into the hundreds. And several UFOs have been sighted in and around the reservoir. According to one UFO sightings database, a Petersham man standing on the eastern shore of the reservoir in April 1996 spotted three UFOs over the water. He reported: "I saw them moving in a circular, sweeping sort of motion. They made no noise and produced only a brightening light that seemed to silhouette them against the sky. . . . The objects were moving at what I would say was thirty miles per hour in a north-south rotation, switching directions in the air. I watched them for about five minutes until the objects zipped over the hills to the west."

Ghosts, aliens, and strange animals living outside of their natural habitats—it's hard to sort out fact from fiction when so many bizarre stories come from just one location. But knowing there are four underwater towns that once bustled with activity, and seeing the remnants of those ghost towns when you look beneath the glassy surface, makes it all seem more believable. The truth is out there somewhere . . . if not in the night sky, then in the depths of the Quabbin Reservoir. Just pray it doesn't reach up from its watery grave and pull you in!

New England's Day of Darkness

The darkness brought on by the eclipse of May 29, 1780, was nothing compared with the darkness that befell the Eastern Seaboard ten days earlier. On that curious morning, New England residents awoke to a bright, sunny day. But on the western horizon, a heavy haze filled the sky, and the thick cloud was moving quickly toward the northeast. By 1:00 in the afternoon, it had become so dark over the entire state of Massachusetts that visibility was a mere several inches. Panic set in as residents became certain that Judgment Day was upon them. Schools were dismissed in Central Massachusetts (and probably elsewhere), and lanterns and candles were lit along streets and in every home, their flames outlined by a curious green aura. Farm animals could sense something unusual going on and behaved unpredictably. People gathered in churches seeking last-minute forgiveness for their sins and praying mightily.

Maybe their prayers saved them, because a blood red full moon finally emerged from the darkness high in the sky at 1:00 in the morning. Twinkling stars quickly followed, and by dawn, the sun was as bright as it had been twenty-four hours before. The fourteen hours of darkness that fell over New England has never been explained.

The Andreasson Alien Encounter

A famous case of alien abduction happened to one of Massachusetts' own, Mrs. Betty (Andreasson) Luca, then of South Ashburnham. It was a cold winter's night in 1967, when the Andreasson home was plunged into darkness just after dinnertime. Betty was in the kitchen and noticed a reddish light shining in through the kitchen window. While she calmed her seven young and understandably frightened children, her father went right up to the window to see what was casting the strange glow. That was when he saw "them." It was an Encounter of the First Kind (when a UFO is in close proximity of the experiencer) and Third Kind (when aliens are visible). Within the next several hours, the family experienced all five known classifications of encounters.

Before Betty's stunned father could even divert his gaze from the surreal scene in the yard, the grayish blue beings that were hopping toward the house seconds before had floated inside, right through a wooden door, and the entire family was immediately put into a state of suspended animation. Paralysis to humans is one of the criteria for Encounters of the Second Kind. Later, under hypnosis, Betty described the beings as only about four feet tall. Their heads were large in proportion to their slight bodies, and their eyes were large, black, and emotionless. Their ears, noses, and mouths were very delicate; in fact, their mouths were mere slits. One of the five aliens telepathically communicated with Betty (Encounter of the Fifth Kind) and assured her that the children would be fine in their trancelike state. Betty was then taken out to the UFO (Encounter of the Fourth Kind) and was returned to her home four hours later, unaware of what had happened to her during those "lost hours."

Eight years later, Dr. J. Allen Hynek advertised that he was seeking true abduction stories from the general public. Betty responded, remembering the red light through the window and the aliens entering her house, as did her father, but that was all they remembered. Because of the large response to the ad, Betty's letter got overlooked and set on the back burner until two years later, when the doctor finally assigned a team to investigate the Andreasson case. It included electronics and aerospace engineers, a solar physicist, a telecommunications specialist, a hypnotist, a medical doctor and psychiatrist, and a UFO investigator. The investigation, which included extensive background and character reference checks, several lie-detector tests, and fourteen lengthy and detailed hypnotic regressions, concluded that nobody involved was fabricating the story. Betty Andreasson and her family were found to be sane individuals who had no motive to lie.

Under many grueling hours of hypnosis (grueling for both hypnotist and subject), Betty was as astonished as anyone to learn that she'd been abducted several times since childhood. Each time, she'd been taken aboard the alien craft and physically examined.

Her alien abductors erased her abduction memories using hypnosis until the right time came to recall her ordeal. She'd been subjected to nasal implants and robotic examinations, but the aliens were never intentionally cruel. In fact, they often reassured her when she became distressed.

She was taken to an alien world, where she was shown a series of symbols, such as a phoenix that rose from the ashes and morphed into a giant gray worm. Such unusual recollections caused a few skeptics to suggest that Betty's experiences were hallucinatory, but she maintains that they were messages from spirit—from God, or "the One," as the aliens called Him. She had experiences similar to religious ecstasy during her abductions—and displayed the same ecstasy during hypnosis. Some wondered if she was actually having religious experiences, rather than true alien encounters. But who's to say the two can't sometimes be related?

The bottom line is that Betty Andreasson's abductions were special. In fact, her abductors had told her since she was a child that she was special and would carry a special message to share with the world. The message was that mankind was on a dangerous course, and unconditional love was required to gain knowledge through spirit. A year after the investigation began, a 528-page report was issued on the Andreasson Encounter, and it became one of the most well-documented and convincing cases in the field of UFOlogy.

The Possession of Maurice Theriault

All cases of demonic possession are bizarre and unnerving. Demons make people do the unthinkable. Thankfully, such incidents are relatively rare, and most towns will never bear witness to a possessed member of their own community. But the town of Warren did. The story made news nationwide and is the subject of a book called *Satan's Harvest* by reporters Michael Lasalandra and Mark Merenda.

The only thing worse than Maurice Theriault's childhood was the condition it left him in as an adult. His father purportedly practiced devil worship and forced his perverse transgressions on his son at an early age. To make matters worse, Maurice was pulled out of school and never obtained more than a third-grade education. One fateful day, Maurice's father confessed to his wife that he and Maurice were both possessed before killing her; then he shot himself in the mouth. Maurice was left to bear the burden of what he had witnessed . . . and the same sad legacy. Like his father, the young Theriault began to display signs and symptoms of demonic possession, and he underwent several unsuccessful exorcisms.

The second exorcism performed on Maurice Theriault, which was recorded on a home videotape in 1985, showed the unspeakable torment the man endured in the latter days of his life. The tape has been shown to scores of incredulous viewers throughout the world as a modern-day example of demonic possession. Many believe it offers indisputable proof of a truly possessed man, but others—even after viewing the sensational tape—believe Theriault suffered from a combination of mental and physical conditions, undoubtedly exacerbated by his horrific childhood experiences. In the tape, Theriault's eyes are already pooling with blood when the actual exorcism begins. The video shows the agonized man's face contorting as his skin splits open on his forehead, boils appear under his skin while the priest speaks in Latin, and bloody drool drips down his chin, staining his white shirt. At one point, he is instructed to blink several times before his glazed-over eyes remain open for at least three minutes straight. During that time, some say his eyes appear "serpentlike," with slits for pupils like a snake or cat. When asked questions by the priest performing the exorcism, Theriault answers in backward Latin—an unbelievable feat for a man who, at best, spoke only broken English. Then his eyes roll back in his head.

It was a five-star performance by a poor, uneducated tomato farmer. But he was no actor, and there was no happy ending to his story. Following in his father's footsteps, Maurice Theriault eventually took his own life, leaving an inquiring public to decide how much of his story was fact and how much, if any, was fabricated.

The Ghost Mill

In 1825, during the birth of the industrial revolution in America, Robert Rogerson built the Crown Mill in the town of North Uxbridge. At one time, roughly two hundred men and women labored under the grandfatherly eye of Rogerson, who was a fair and selfless boss. But in 1840, Rogerson went bankrupt and was forced to sell the mill, leaving the same employees in the hands of the greedy new owners, who had no concern for their laborers. For eighty-three years, the textile mill continued to operate, in spite of the increasing despair felt by its hardworking employees. It finally closed in 1923 and stood vacant and untouched until a fire destroyed it in 1974—in the midst of efforts to have the mill purchased and preserved as a historic site in a proposed state park in Blackstone Valley.

The mill had been reported to be haunted even before the fire. People had seen sad, gaunt faces in the upper windows and watched apparitions of mill workers come and go through the main entrance, as if continuing with their daily routine. Many locals felt strange sensations while passing by the mill grounds, as though they were being watched from the numerous windows in the abandoned structure. But the most perplexing phenomenon occurred in the wake of the fire. Even though the mill no longer stands, it has been known to appear *solidly* before people—hence its nickname, the "ghost mill."

One man, as reported in Charles Turek Robinson's New England Ghost Files, came upon the mill while out for a walk in 1975—a year after it burned down. He knew nothing of the mill or its history, but it looked interesting, and he couldn't resist the temptation to get a closer look. Once inside, he noted that the structure seemed sound, but it was too dark to explore, so he headed for the door. On his way out, he was attacked by a man wielding a long piece of wood. He ducked to miss the swing, and when he looked back up, his faceless intruder was gone. He quickly left and reported the incident to the police. That was when his day got even weirder. The police informed him that the mill he spoke of had burned down the year before (they must have thought they had a real live one there!). The man returned to the site and was disappointed to discover that the mill was, indeed, nowhere to be found, just as the police had said. He might have felt better knowing that he wasn't the only one who came upon the ghost mill. Others had seen the mill still standing in the months after it burned down, as well. Luckily for them, they resisted the urge to enter the apparitional building and thus saved themselves from being accosted by the club-wielding phantom.

Apple-Loving Alien Craft

The deer aren't the only creatures looking for apples in the orchards of Lunenburg. On August 12, 2002, a man and his son saw something extraordinary outside of their farmhouse—a UFO. The man's first thought was that he was looking at some sort of cutting-edge device used to spray the orchards, but then the spinning, cone-shaped object took a sharp turn and darted away, effectively negating that idea. He and his eight-year-old son visually tracked the object for several minutes, and both agreed that it was three to six feet tall and moved much faster than any aircraft they'd ever seen. The man was able to grab his digital camera, but the object had already moved about a half mile away, so the photographs revealed only a small dot in several frames; however, the triangular shape of the object was apparent when the dot was zoomed in on.

No other sightings of that nature were reported that night to local law enforcement offices, the Federal Aviation Administration, or the National Weather Service. And although the man doesn't know what he saw, he does know what he *didn't* see—it definitely wasn't a meteor, as was suggested by some. It doesn't take a rocket scientist to determine that meteors don't hover over apple orchards and dart about erratically. Incidentally, the town of Lunenburg is adjacent to Fitchburg—widely considered to be "UFO Central" of the state of Massachusetts. Coincidence? I think not.

The New England Airship Invasion of 1909

Fitchburg featured prominently in the "New England Airship Invasion" of 1909. On December 22 of that year, more than thirty towns and cities in Massachusetts were visited by UFOs. An estimated ten thousand people throughout New England witnessed a large, cigar-shaped aircraft that sometimes zigzagged and sometimes hovered—but at no time acted like any aircraft anyone had ever seen. In downtown Boston, people stopped their wagons and stood in the streets gaping up at the sky.

Apparently the object followed a train from Boston to Fitchburg, because the next day, the Evening Limited steam locomotive made history when it encountered the brazen craft. According to an article in the December 24, 1909, Fitchburg *Sentinel:* "Like fire the word went around that the mysterious airship that startled Worcester the night before was hovering over the city. Over the peak of Rollstone Hill a wonderfully bright light glowed, and hundreds watched it with wonder, not unmixed with awe."

The article continued: "A messenger on a train westbound out of Boston first saw the airship at Ayer, when it came down from the west to meet the train. The messenger is a violent convert to the airship theory. He says the powerful light of the ship was played upon the cars of the train, and it followed along until (Fitchburg) was reached. Then it temporarily disappeared and was not picked up again until the train got up the line, and for some time the light played over and around the cars."

A self-proclaimed inventor from Worcester, taking advantage of the exceptional situation, claimed to have built the airship, but his statements proved fraudulent. The objects seen were much larger and more technologically advanced than anything that could have been flown in 1909, and the opportunist never produced the so-called aircraft to prove his claim.

UFOs have been reported over Fitchburg in nearly every decade since the "invasion" of 1909, with the 1950s and 1970s being particularly active. Fitchburg's most recent sighting was in 1996; however, in nearby Lunenburg, a father and son saw a UFO over their apple orchard as recently as 2002. The entire area is still considered active.

North Shore

THE NORTH SHORE REGION INCLUDES THE LEGENDARY FISHING PORT OF Gloucester, where *The Perfect Storm* was filmed; world-famous sailing harbors such as Marblehead; and the shipbuilding capitals of Newburyport, Essex, Cape Ann, and Salem. Ah, Salem—we can't forget that one, can we? Salem is the setting of novelist Nathaniel Hawthorne's *House of the Seven Gables,* and it's also the home of the witch trials, so you can imagine how many restless spirits are floating around. The North Shore stretches along the rocky coastline from immediately north of Boston to the northernmost tip of the state, which is why much of its local lore involves giant sea monsters, sunken ships, ill-fated sea captains meeting untimely demises, and haunted caverns along the shoreline. With so much murder and mayhem, is it any wonder more stories are included from this region than any other?

Mammy Red of Marblehead

In the dangerous period of delusion known as the Salem Witch-Hunt, the Puritans of seventeenth-century Salem so strongly believed that Satan had infiltrated their fledgling settlement that they trusted nobody . . . not their neighbors, not their clergy, and sometimes not even their own flesh and blood. The Dark One, most believed, had endowed riches and wizardry upon all who succumbed to his temptation. In return, they promised him their eternal souls. Anyone who behaved strangely—hearing voices, seeing spirits, or speaking in tongues—or professed any unusual ability, such as divination, premonition, or the gift of healing, was considered to be in partnership with the Devil himself. Today such abilities are considered "spiritual gifts" from God, and we embrace them. But in old Salem, those so-called gifts were both feared and loathed. The bearers faced accusations of practicing witchcraft, and it was widely assumed that they had sold their souls to the Devil to obtain their unnatural powers. Far-fetched suspicions and accusations resulted in a widespread baseless hysteria.

Poor old Mammy Red of Marblehead. She was labeled a witch out of pure convenience and ignorance. Disgusted by puritanical pomposity, she glowered at her neighbors bitterly during those volatile times, but some took her glare to be the dreaded "evil eye." Who better to blame the wave of paranormal occurrences on? *Someone* had to be blamed and brought to justice. Even two dogs were accused of "giving the evil eye" and hanged for their crimes. Many undeserving souls met the same fate during the witch hysteria. But aside from glaring at passersby, what exactly were Mammy's crimes?

According to author Charles M. Skinner (1852–1907) in *Myths and Legends of Our Own Land: Tales of Puritan Land,* the locals believed she was responsible for a long list of "queer happenings." As Skinner explained:

> Ships had appeared just before they were wrecked and had vanished while people looked at them; men were seen walking on the water after they had been comfortably buried; the wind was heard to name the sailors doomed never to return; footsteps and voices were heard in the streets before the great were to die; one man was chased by a corpse in its coffin; another was pursued by the devil in a carriage drawn by four white horses; a young woman who had just received a present of some fine fish from her lover was amazed to see him melt into the air and was heartbroken when she learned the next morning that he had died at sea. So far away as Amesbury the devil's power was shown by the appearance of a man who walked the roads carrying his head under his arm, and by the freak of a windmill that the miller always used to shut up at sundown, but that started itself at midnight.

Clearly, the townspeople were experiencing a great deal of ghost-related phenomena. They were being *haunted,* not bewitched. But that discrepancy was recognized more than three hundred years too late for the condemned Mammy Red of Marblehead, who was hanged for a multitude of frightful deeds that she had nothing at all to do with.

Witches, and Warlocks, and Devils . . . Oh My!

The witch hysteria of old New England took hold in 1692, with the first accused being a wild Irishwoman named Glover who lived in Danvers. Word spread like wildfire to the neighboring community of Salem, and the rest is history—but it still bears repeating here, because it is the source of much legend and conjecture.

Though in actuality their deeds were trivial, if anything at all, witches were quickly blamed for anything and everything. They were alleged to cause disease to livestock, blight of crops, aches and pains and illnesses to both young and old, and pricking (remotely) of small children with pins and thorns. Indeed, the word of a child was enough reason to hang, burn, or drown a witch—if the executioners were brave enough to pay the possible consequences for their hasty actions. Often witches who admitted their guilt were either imprisoned or set free, rather than executed, on account of the possibility that they would cast evil spells on their executioners.

So outrageous was the popular belief that the Devil had somehow coerced the citizens of the community into selling their souls and practicing witchcraft that New Englanders even went so far as to hang a child of five and a dog or two. Gallows Hill saw many sad and unjust tragedies, and the old elm tree that stood on Boston Common until 1876 was said to have served as a gallows both for witches and for Quakers who stepped out of line. A kindred hysteria hung over the region like a dark cloud, and nobody was safe from twisted accusations. Often the accusers became the accused, and the victims became the victimizers.

Many Salemites who had fallen under suspicion fled to far-off towns, rather than risk an accusation that could lead to their death.

One such woman, a fair maiden from Wenham, was rescued by her lover from the jail in which she'd been incarcerated. He then planted her safely among the Quakers near the Merrimac. A Miss Wheeler of Salem was quickly whisked away by her brothers when she fell under suspicion. They rowed around Cape Ann and delivered her safely to the "witch house" at Pigeon Cove.

When Philip English's wife was arrested, he asked to share her fate, so both were shuffled to Boston, where they had the unusual arrangement of spending their days as free citizens and their nights in jail. Before their trial date in Salem, they went to church and heard the Reverend Joshua Moody say, "If they persecute ye in one city, flee thee unto another." With that, the sensible clergyman opened the jail door where the Englishes were imprisoned, allowing the unfortunate pair to escape to New York. They remained there until the majority of people in Salem came to their senses, and then they safely returned. Mrs. English died shortly after her return to Salem from the anxiety of her ordeal, and the good and wise Reverend Moody found it necessary to move to Plymouth to escape the wrath of those few who couldn't let the famous witch hunt go. Even though the witch hunt had died down, many still harbored doubts and erroneous fears, especially when confronted with any unusual circumstance, as in the following account by Charles Skinner in his *Myths and Legends of Our Own Land* series:

In the Merrimac Valley the devil found converts for many years after: Goody Mose, of Rocks Village, who tumbled downstairs when a big beetle was killed at an evening party some miles away after it had been bumping into the faces of the company; Goody Whitcher, of Amesbury, whose loom kept banging day and night after she was dead; Goody Sloper, of West Newbury, who went home lame directly after a man had struck his axe into the beam of a house that she had bewitched, but who recovered her strength and established an improved reputation when, in 1794, she swam out to a capsized boat and rescued two of the people who were in peril; Goodman Nichols, of Rocks Village, who "spelled" a neighbor's son, compelling him to run up one end of the house, along the ridge, and down the other end, "troubling the family extremely by his strange proceedings"; Susie Martin, also of Rocks, who was hanged, in spite of her devotions in jail, though the rope danced so that it could not be tied, but a crow overhead called for a withe, and the law was executed with that; and Goody Morse, of Market and High Streets, Newburyport, whose baskets and pots danced through her house continually and who was seen "flying about the sun as if she had been cut in twain, or as if the devil did hide the lower part of her."

There's no doubt that old New England had its share of weird happenings that were easier to pin on a witch than to try to figure out otherwise.

The Curse of the Charles Haskell

The *Charles Haskell* was damned before it ever made its maiden voyage. The schooner was built in 1869 for cod fishing and was in the midst of its final inspection when tragedy struck on board. A workman slipped on the deck and broke his neck. The fatality doomed the *Haskell* to misfortune and infamy, for it was considered a very bad omen to have a death on board before a ship's first voyage. Considering the circumstances, the man who would have been captain wisely refused to sail her. So strong was the public belief in such sinister omens, in fact, that nobody came forward and offered to take the unchristened ship out. Nobody, that is, until a man named Captain Curtis of Gloucester accepted the challenge a year later. And he lived to regret it—but at least he lived.

The *Haskell*'s first winter at sea proved to be especially harsh. One day, a hurricane struck while dozens of fishing vessels, including the ill-fated *Charles Haskell*, were positioned off the rich fishing grounds of Georges Bank. The *Haskell* was thrown against the *Andrew Johnson* in the chaos, and even though both ships were damaged, only the *Johnson* went down, along with all hands on board. Twenty-six seamen were lost to the curse of the *Charles Haskell*, though the *Haskell*'s own crew was spared. The insidious schooner crept back to port, where she would be repaired in time for the bountiful spring season.

In the spring of 1870, the curse reared its ugly head once again. The first five days at sea had been mercifully uneventful, but on the sixth evening, something happened that was so distressing to the crew that the *Haskell* would return uncharacteristically early to port. Two crewmen were on the midnight watch when they saw the apparitions of a couple dozen men in oilskins silently climbing over the rails. Their eyes were empty sockets. Captain Curtis came out to see what the commotion was about, and he, too, saw the intrusive specters. The phantom fishermen took up their positions along the fishing benches and cast invisible fishing lines out over the water. Then, as mysteriously as they'd appeared, they stood up precisely and walked back to the railing, climbed over the side, and disappeared into the vast, dark sea. Captain Curtis wasted no time turning his clearly haunted ship toward home, but he knew he and his crew would have to endure one more night at sea before reaching Gloucester Harbor.

The following night, as feared, the scene repeated itself, but with a twist on its final act. Once again, the phantom seamen climbed on board and set to work. But this time, when they were finished fishing, they climbed overboard and walked silently on the water—in single file, no less—toward Salem. The *Charles Haskell* never sailed again. Because of the ghost tales, nobody would go anywhere near her. Eventually, the jinxed schooner decomposed at her final resting place in the harbor, ironically—yet befittingly—just like the twenty-six restless souls she had mercilessly sent to the ocean floor.

Hawthorne Hotel

The six-story Hawthorne Hotel at 18 Washington Square West in Salem was completed in 1925 to accommodate the growing number of visitors to the community. The stately structure is located "on the Common," surrounded by historic buildings in the Common Historic District—the heart of Salem. If it hadn't been for the generosity of the sea captains who made up the Salem Marine Society in the 1920s, the hotel wouldn't even be there. The society's original building was built in 1766 and was razed for construction of the hotel, but a small building with nautical decor was added up on the rooftop of the hotel for the society to use as headquarters and a meeting place; it was a condition of the property sale.

There's something fishy going on where the Salem Marine Society first planted its roots. It seems some old sea captains may still linger on the property. The heavy nautical theme throughout must make them feel right at home. Charts and records stored in the society's headquarters on the roof have been found in disarray, even though the building is kept locked at all times. In what was once the Main Brace Restaurant (now Nathaniels) at the hotel, there was a large ship's wheel that seemed to move of its own volition. It turned back and forth right before the eyes of customers and employees, and if anyone tried to stop its mysterious motion, it simply continued after they stepped away. The lower deck has the appearance of an actual ship's interior. One employee refused to work alone in the room after leaving for only a moment and returning to find tables and chairs he'd just set up turned in the exact opposite direction.

One of the hotel's 89 rooms—Room 325, to be exact—appears to have been haunted, at least at one time. A guest who stayed in the room, a suite with two bedrooms and one bathroom, told the front desk clerk that he didn't realize he'd have to share his bath with another customer. He was insistent that he had heard someone in the bathroom, and that whoever it was had closed his own door to the bathroom. He could see the light shining through the cracks around the door, and he could hear the water running and the toilet flush. So adamant was the customer that the desk clerk escorted him back up to his room and showed him the layout, assuring him again that there was only one access to his room, and he had the only key. Once the idea of sharing his room with a ghost sank in, the man decided to stay in the room for a week.

The League of Specters

Gloucester has seen some pretty strange things, but one of the strangest things of all was the noisy arrival in 1692 of a league of Frenchmen and Indians that couldn't be caught, killed, or even injured—even though two regiments of Gloucester men went into Cape Ann and battled them for two weeks. It was said that the windows of Plymouth rattled with the passage of the unseen horsemen. What's more, the mysterious league's arrival was marked by the simultaneous appearance of what looked like an Indian bow and scalp on the face of the moon.

It didn't take long to realize that these men were not of flesh and blood. The colonists were sure they were devils wishing to bring "moral perversion" to New England. Everyone witnessed the apparition for two weeks, though Cape Ann remained on guard against "the specter leaguers" for years, because the town had no idea what or whom it was up against or when they might return. And return they did . . .

Late one summer night after the noisy battle with the phantoms had ended, Ebenezer Babson was returning home when he saw two men run from his house and disappear into the swamp. When his family told him moments later that they'd had no visitors, he assumed they were prowlers up to no good, so he ran out the door after them. On his approach, the two jumped up from behind a log, and he heard one say, "The master of the house is now come, else we might have taken the house." Then they vanished again, even deeper into the swamp.

For several nights, the men appeared, wearing white breeches and waistcoats and carrying bright guns. But somehow they couldn't be caught. Neither could the many phantoms whose footsteps were heard during the same time on the grounds of the barracks. Babson thought he might get lucky on July 4, when at least six similarly dressed specters appeared and the real soldiers had them surrounded. Remarkably, Babson brought three of "ye unaccountable troublers" to the ground with just one lucky shot (and a very real bullet whizzed past his ear from one of the real troops in the exchange). As Babson and his men approached the spot where the alleged phantoms lay, they stood up and raced off into the woods as if nothing had happened to them. As they ran, one of them was felled again by gunfire, but when Babson's men picked him up, he melted into the air. At that moment, a "fierce jabbering in an unknown tongue" was said to have emanated throughout the swamp, presumably by the incensed league of specters.

Later, a man named Richard Dolliver came upon eleven of them huddled and chanting. He scattered them with a gunshot, but the elusive lot could not be brought down. Terror fell on the people of Cape Ann for the better part of a month, and word was out that Satan was ambushing the good people of Gloucester with demons in the form of armed Indians and Frenchmen. To say that all hell broke loose would be quite appropriate. Stones flew about, barns were battered, and people often heard the marching of unseen soldiers after dark. At one point, the brazen troublemakers went right up to Babson, stared defiantly down the barrel of his gun, and laid a charm on it that made it flash in the pan each time he shot it at them.

Neighboring troops were brought in, but it was no use. Battling with the phantoms was futile, or so it seemed. Then one night, the shameless and hostile league emerged from the swamp and moved toward the barracks where twenty soldiers and their captain were keeping guard. The captain was determined to end the insanity and said, "If you be ghosts or devils, I will foil you." He then tore one single silver button from his doublet, rammed it into his gun, and fired at the approaching league. With that, the untouchable army vanished. The effect of the silver "bullet" proved to the people that the leaguers were not "of human kind" but were of the Devil. Later that evening, just as the weary townspeople began to feel confident that their ordeal had finally ended, a cry went out that the demons were returning. This time, with no other options at their disposal, the village's soldiers laid their guns aside, sank to their knees, and prayed. If they were truly at war with the Devil, the power of prayer was the only effective weapon. As the name of God was uttered, the marching sound ended, and angry howls rang out from the atmosphere surrounding the village. It was the sound of good conquering evil. At long last, the evil leaguers had finally been vanquished.

The Shrieking Englishwoman

In the late 1600s, a rich Spanish ship was commandeered off Marblehead by merciless English pirates, who killed every person on board but one—a beautiful English lady passenger. Hers was a more prolonged and savage death than that of her fellow passengers and crew. The pirates brought her ashore under the cover of darkness and brutally beat her at a ledge of rocks near Oakum Bay. With that dirty deed done, they dragged her battered, nearly lifeless body a little way from shore in their boat and tossed her overboard. To their surprise, she came to the surface and clutched the side of the boat, crying, "Lord, save me! Mercy! Oh, Lord Jesus, save me!" The pirates hacked at her hands with heavy swords until her fingers were severed. Then she slipped beneath the surface, and the sickening screams that had filled the night were at once replaced by an unnatural, sorrowful silence.

The women and children of Marblehead had been awakened by the poor Englishwoman's startling shrieks as her life was being taken from her, but they were too afraid to help. Their husbands were fishermen and were away in their boats, and the women and children didn't dare attempt a rescue without them, lest they themselves become victims. The woman's mangled body, as expected, washed up on the rocks where her brutal ordeal had begun. The people cursed the beasts that had done this to her and gave her a proper English burial in the spot where her body was found.

The victim's cries and appeals continued to be heard for nearly two hundred years on each anniversary of the crime, when her spirit returned to the scene. Her haunting voice was so clear and loud that it was unmistakable, and most of the citizens of Marblehead were said to have heard it at least once over the course of those two centuries.

The Gloucester Sea Serpent

Ah, the mysterious sea serpent. Science says such a creature does not exist; but then, science questions the legitimacy of ghosts, no matter how much evidence is presented in support of their existence. Is it such a far stretch to imagine that a creature somewhat akin to the mighty Anaconda, yet surpassing it in size, can dwell in the depths of our oceans and lakes? Many respectable citizens along the Atlantic shores have reported seeing "giant sea snakes" over the past several hundred years, from the earliest reported sighting in seventeenth-century Cape Ann to the last known sighting far up north in Newfoundland at the close of the twentieth century.

It's true that the vast majority of sightings along the Massachusetts coast occurred in the 1800s, when hoaxes ran rampant in journalism, yet many reports were from respectable and sound sources, such as the *Boston Weekly Messenger* and the *American Journal of Science and Arts*. Others were taken from personal correspondence never intended for public viewing, effectively eliminating the likelihood of hoaxes and sensationalism. But why have the sightings markedly decreased in the past hundred years? Some speculate that it's because the fishing grounds off the coast of northern Massachusetts no longer have the abundant food supply the sea serpent once relied upon. The ecosystem has been thrown off by years of heavy fishing, leaving the ancient serpent with no choice but to move farther out to sea—and thus farther out of sight—in search of more fertile feeding grounds, rather than face extinction.

The first recorded sighting, in 1638, was reported by John Josselyn: "They told me of a sea serpent, or snake, that lay quoiled up like a cable upon the rock at Cape Ann; a boat passing by with English on board, and two Indians, they would have shot the serpent, but the Indians dissuaded them, saying that if he were not killed outright, they would all be in danger of their lives." Three years later, Obadiah Turner reported a creature off the coast of Lynn: "Some being on ye great beach gathering of clams and seaweed which had been cast thereon by ye mighty storm did spy a most wonderful serpent a short way off from ye shore. He was big round in ye thickest part as a wine pipe; and they do affirm that he was fifteen fathoms or more in length."

Many personal accounts of sightings were gathered in 1817 by the New England Linnaean Society, a group charged with getting to the bottom of the sea serpent rumor. Sightings reached their all-time annual high that year, with eighteen cases being reported. The vast majority of the society's witnesses agreed that the Gloucester creature resembled a serpent, because of its up-and-down manner of motion and its snakelike appearance. It was typically said to be brown, sixty to one hundred feet long, jointed from head to tail, and about the width of a barrel. It moved rapidly in a "serpentine fashion" and was sometimes reported to have a long, pointed horn on its head. Its head has been compared to that of many animals—dogs, sea turtles, horses, and snakes—with the size of the head proportioned to the size of the body.

One credible and knowledgeable witness, Cheever Felch, who encountered the serpent while aboard the USS *Science,* told the society:

> His colour is dark brown with white under his throat. His size we could not accurately ascertain. . . . We did not see his tail; but from the end of the head to the farthest protuberance was not far from one hundred feet. I speak with a degree of certainty, being much accustomed to measure and estimate distances and length. I counted fourteen bunches on his back, the first one say ten or twelve feet from his head, and the others about seven feet apart. They decreased in size towards the tail. . . . His motion was partly vertical and partly horizontal, like that of fresh-water snakes. I have been much acquainted with snakes in our interior waters. His motion was the same.

Throughout recorded history, details of sea serpent reports have remained consistently alike, whether in reference to Loch Ness's "Nessie," Lake Champlain's "Champ," Lake Okanagan's "Ogopogo," or Gloucester's own "Great New England Sea Serpent." After hundreds of eyewitness accounts over the course of several hundred years, the sea serpent deserves more than just a chapter in the annals of cryptozoology.

Castle of the Damned

The illustrious John Hays Hammond Jr. was certainly no couch potato, but he did invent the remote control—one of his more than 800 inventions. He patented 426 inventions at his castle at 80 Hesperus Avenue in Gloucester. In fact, one of the reasons he built the medieval-style castle in 1926 was to house the Hammond Research Corporation. Besides being a prolific inventor, second only to Thomas Edison, Hammond was also an ardent collector of historic items that transported him, if only by mind, to other places and times. The castle would showcase his treasures while providing adequate space to bring into reality the objects of his dreams.

John Hammond's passion for transcending time, and why it was so important for him to collect and surround himself with remnants of the past, is revealed in the following excerpt of an unpublished 1929 letter found on the Hammond Castle website:

> For the last three years I motored many miles through Europe. After traveling all day, I would arrive at my destination to see a church, a cathedral, a town hall, a scrap of Roman wall or viaduct, a coliseum or an ancient theatre. It was always a piece of architecture that suddenly dissipated the obscurity of time and brought the living presence back of all ages. It is in the stones and wood that the personal record of man comes down to us. We call it atmosphere, this indescribable something that still haunts old monuments. You can read history, you can visit a hundred museums containing the handiwork, but nothing can reincarnate their spirit except to walk through rooms in which they have lived and through the scenes that were the background of their lives. It is a marvelous thing, this expression of human ideals in walls and windows.

According to John Pettibone, executive director and curator of the Hammond Museum Inc., Hammond's "very strong belief was that, as a collector of history, you bring back the spirit of the original owners of objects, and he was very respectful of those spirits."

Some of the objects on display in the castle—now owned and operated by the nonprofit Museum Trust—are medieval and Gothic artifacts, genuine Renaissance furniture, early American furnishings, and Roman tombstones embedded on the wall of a church front on the property. Visitors touring the castle may see all of that . . . and more, if they're lucky. Some say the castle is haunted by the spirit of Hammond himself—that his soft-soled shoes are still heard walking across the stone floor. Perhaps the man who dreamed of transcending time and space managed to realize his dream. He always said he'd come back as a cat, and Pettibone admits he has seen a lot of cats visit the castle from out of the woods in his twenty-one years of working there. (He always nods his head and says hello to the animals, just in case.)

Another interesting object on the property is the Azteclike tomb Hammond had built for himself years before his death in 1965. Pettibone said Hammond occasionally had lunch on the roof of his tomb, then grabbed the keys to the tomb and eagerly asked his guests if they wanted to see where he would be buried. For some reason, Hammond also had locks put on the inside of the main door to his tomb. Pettibone wonders, "Do you think he wanted to let himself out every now and then?"

Rumors of Hammond's ghost are propagated by the popular haunted house attraction held each year throughout the month of October on the grounds of the castle, dubbed "Castle of the Damned" for the event. The dungeons, drawbridge, looming stone towers, eerily silent chambers, and tombstone-embedded walls certainly set the tone. Make-believe phantoms are eager to pounce out at unsuspecting victims, so don't let your guard down! But if you hear soft footfalls, the ghost of Hammond himself may be overseeing the festivities. After all, Halloween was Hammond's favorite holiday. He even named one of his cats "Boo." That's what he said to guests in his castle, after sneaking up behind them and tapping them on their shoulders.

Since starting their annual Halloween Haunted Nights in the mid-eighties, the staff has had a feeling that Hammond joins them for the revelry from time to time. They would like to think so. They're not the only ones who feel a genuine spirit presence in the castle. According to Pettibone: "A surgical trauma nurse got as far as the bottom of the stairs leading into the Great Hall and returned to the lobby in tears, saying, 'I deal with life and death every day, and there is something in this place that scares me.' I refunded her admission on the spot as she moved quickly to the front door." Apparently, Hammond continues to sneak up behind his guests to say, "Boo!"

Swallow Cave

Just north of Boston, along the rocky shoreline of Nahant Island, is a grotto called Swallow Cave, aptly named for its massive swallow population throughout much of the year. The five-foot-tall mouth of the ample cave was the site of a blood-sparing truce masterminded by a witch named Wonderful in 1675. The seventy-year-old Wonderful was brilliant and likable—not the stereotypical witch of the era—but she was called a witch because of her uncanny ability to find lost objects and predict future events. And that's why a captain and two dozen soldiers from Lynn consulted her on their way to hunt down and slaughter forty Narragansett warriors who had raided their town two weeks earlier.

Wonderful knew who was knocking on her door that dark and dismal night, even before she opened it—that's why she got paid big money! She knew what they were there for, and she knew the answers she would give. When a band of vengeful Indians from Pocasset invaded Lynn to express their outrage at their land and homes being taken by the white man, they were met by the men of Lynn, who struck back, overcoming the Indians and forcing them to retreat to the beach. The captain and his men had lost the trail of the fleeing Indians but vowed to find them and destroy those who had gotten away. They spent the next two weeks preparing for battle, while the Indians camped out near the shore, sharpening their tomahawks and planning their own surprise attack. And Wonderful was formulating her own plan, along with a catchy little jingle:

> Mingle, mingle, mingle, mingle,
> Away, apart, together, single,
> The Indians on the shore you'll see.
> Your death or life—remember me.

Wonderful told the captain and his men that they would find the Indians they sought on the Nahant shore, hiding in wait. The men left at once to find them. Near a place called Forty Steps, the captain told his men to lie low and motionless—an Indian was nearby. The Indian saw the captain at the same time and sounded an alert to another Indian who was on guard. But under the cover of darkness, it was easy for both sides to escape unseen. When the captain finally ventured out to see what the Indians were up to, he found himself on a cliff high above Swallow Cave, looking down on two Indians who were bragging about how they planned to kill everyone in Lynn the next day. Just as the enraged captain raised his musket, he heard the voice of Wonderful behind him. She had known this was going to happen, of course.

Wonderful told the captain he would regret it if he killed them, and she promised she could make the Indians surrender without bloodshed. After consulting with the Indians in the cave alone, Wonderful came out with the one who seemed to be in charge and cut a deal with the captain from Lynn. If he would let the Indians retrieve their hidden canoes and return to Pocasset, they would solemnly swear to never fight the white man again at Lynn. After careful consideration—and under the watchful eye of Wonderful, who probably wouldn't have allowed them to say no—they agreed. The standoff was over, a peace accord was reached, and Wonderful's job there was done.

Several days later, Wonderful predicted that her own death would soon come. When the soldiers found her body in her hut two weeks later, the grateful citizens of Lynn buried it high on the hill overlooking Swallow Cave. Today, if you see a misty apparition near the mouth of the cave at dusk, as many people have, don't fear. It's just Wonderful, lingering at the spot where she accomplished what might have been her greatest deed.

The Stephen Daniels House

The Stephen Daniels House, at One Daniels Street in Salem, was built in 1667. It holds the distinction of being the longest-operating bed-and-breakfast in the city, and its guest rooms have private baths and are delightfully adorned with antiques, wood-burning fireplaces, and hand-painted portraits. Whether you're admiring

the innkeeper's collection of antiques or sitting in the private, flower-filled English garden, you really are transported back in time to old New England—a time of superstition and paranoia. If actually being in Salem makes you feel more superstitious than usual, you won't have to worry *too* much about the cat that crosses your path at the inn. It doesn't meet the prerequisites for bringing bad luck. For one thing, it's not entirely black, and for another, it's not entirely alive! Still, it never hurts to leave a bowl of milk beside your bed to appease the phantom feline. But you're not afraid of a little kitty, are you?

Kay Gill is the proud owner of the inn today. In 1953, ten years before she bought the inn, she painted a portrait of a gray tabby. When she moved in, she hung the portrait in the Rose Room—the same room her guests tell her is haunted by a gray-and-black-striped cat that looks just like the one in the painting. Another guest swore that he saw an apparition of a man in the dining room that looked just like a portrait on the wall in that room. This then begs the question: Is it the paintings that are haunted, or is it the inn? Kay isn't so sure it's either, but admitted "recently a guest sleeping in the great room had a visit from a man in a shiny black suit and top hat who, from the description, looked remarkably like Stephen Daniels. The man stood there a moment, then said 'welcome to the house.' I always feel that the people who have lived here over the years are happy we are here and that so many people can enjoy their house."

Kay herself has never heard so much as a purr. But her patrons assure her that she does, indeed, have a ghost or two, and that's okay with them. It adds to the charm of staying in an old New England inn. Return customers even remember to leave a bowl of milk out at night, hopeful that they'll once again encounter their furry friend. After all, a visit to an enchanted city like Salem just isn't complete without a supernatural experience.

The House of the Seven Gables

You could just as easily call it the House of the Seven Ghosts, because at least that many have been encountered on the grounds over the years, including the spirit of Susannah Ingersoll, a Victorian boy in the attic, a dressmaker, and maybe even a slave or two.

The House of the Seven Gables is the oldest seventeenth-century wooden mansion still standing in all of New England. Its sprawling grounds make up an entire historic district on the National Register of Historic Places.

The world-famous gabled house at 54 Turner Street on Salem's harbor was built in 1668 and is also known as the Turner-Ingersoll Mansion. The great novelist Nathaniel Hawthorne spent much time visiting his cousin Susannah Ingersoll there. She provided the inspiration for some of his characters and lived in the house until her death at the age of seventy-two. Hawthorne's novel *The House of the Seven Gables* was based in part on his experiences in the home, many of which were paranormal in nature. But the central theme of the novel is ancestral guilt. His great-great-grandfather John Hawthorne was known as "the Hanging Judge" for his involvement in the Salem Witch Trials of 1692, and Nathaniel felt tremendous guilt over this.

According to Don Knuuttila, director of marketing and guest services at the House of the Seven Gables, Hawthorne's novel "begins with Colonel Pyncheon wanting to purchase the land from Matthew Maule, but Maule refuses. Therefore, Colonel Pyncheon declares Maule to be a witch, so Maule is convicted and hanged. Before he is hanged, Maule looks at Pyncheon and says, 'God will give you blood to drink!' A curse then hangs over the Pyncheon house until it is finally broken when Phoebe (a Pyncheon) and Holgrave (a Maule) fall in love generations later." In reality, "the widow Moore owned the property on which the Turner-Ingersoll [Mansion] now stands. John Turner purchased the land and her house. As you can see, Hawthorne used the premise of a true story and fictionalized it. Some scholars also believe that Hebzibah Pyncheon is based on Susannah Ingersoll."

Hawthorne was born in 1804 in a house several blocks away that was later relocated to the grounds. Today visitors can tour his childhood home, said to be haunted by a dressmaker who still sews at a phantom sewing machine and wanders around the house. Many besides Hawthorne have claimed to have encountered ghosts on the grounds of the House of the Seven Gables. Several sources have reported a boy in Victorian clothing in the mansion's attic. Susan Ingersoll's spirit is also believed to linger—or at least the spirit of a woman of similar appearance. Photographs of the windows taken from outdoors have revealed what looks like faces in them. A whole lot of unexplainable clanging and clattering seem to go on throughout the premises, and bathroom fixtures turn on and off of their own accord. Doors open and close, hinges click—all with no assistance from any living person. Most of the ghostly behavior is attributed to the slaves who passed through the house as part of the Underground Railroad.

In such a richly historic place, where there's so much for tourists to see, there's also much that remains unseen: secret passageways, hidden staircases—and ghosts for every gable.

The Joshua Ward House

Someone has a bone to pick at the incredibly haunted Joshua Ward House at 148 Washington Street in Salem, but if it's the evil George Corwin's bones they want, they're barking up the wrong tree. As soon as it was safe for his skeleton to be brought out of the basement beneath the house—many years after his notorious dastardly deeds—his family moved it to the Broad Street Cemetery. That's not to say that his dark soul didn't stay behind in the house, which was built on the foundation of his former dwelling. And it wouldn't be at all surprising if an angry witch or two were hot on his heels.

It all began in 1692, with the crushing death of Giles Corey at the hands of Sheriff George Corwin. Corwin sentenced Corey's wife to death by hanging and insisted that he plead either guilty or innocent to witchcraft. He was trapped. No matter which way he pleaded, he knew he was doomed—either to be hanged for not admitting to being a warlock or sentenced to life in prison for admitting to the crime. Corey "took the Fifth" rather than face certain punishment either way. Too bad the Bill of Rights wouldn't be drawn up for another hundred years. The sly and shameless Corwin found a loophole that would allow him to punish Corey for his disobedience. It was an old English law that permitted the crushing of suspected witches and warlocks if they refused to cooperate with the authorities. The idea was to "squeeze the truth out of them."

And so it was that the elderly Giles Corey was led naked to an open field behind the old Salem jail where he had stood trial and was thrown into a shallow hole. A board was then placed on him, followed by boulder after debilitating boulder, slowly leading to a most gruesome death. The hapless man's last words—which have reverberated throughout history—were directed at Corwin and his so-called men of the law: "Damn you. I curse you and Salem!" And he did. From that day forward, every sheriff stationed at the jail overlooking the "killing grounds" has suffered a disease of the heart or blood or some other mysterious malady, often with a fatal outcome, unless they left office prematurely, as author and former sheriff Robert Cahill did.

Corwin died of a heart attack five years after his most heinous crime. By then he was so widely despised that his family had no choice but to bury him in the basement of his home, rather than run the risk of his tomb being desecrated by an angry populace. His body was interred and his remains moved to a cemetery after things settled down. Then the Joshua Ward federal-style mansion was constructed on the foundation of the detested sheriff's home.

It didn't take the people of Salem long to realize that the Giles Corey curse extended well beyond the confines of the jailhouse, just as he had intended. Corey's scruffy ghost has been seen by many people before various calamities have occurred in Salem, such as the fire that swept through the city in 1914, starting not so coincidentally at Gallows Hill, where so many alleged witches had met horrific fates at the hands of Sheriff Corwin. Corey's skeletal apparition precedes such events, typically drifting about near the Howard Street Burying Ground. It's no wonder Howard Street is known as "the most haunted street in Salem." There are a lot of very unsettled souls drifting about, not the least being Corey himself.

If Howard Street is the most haunted street in Salem, the Joshua Ward House, currently owned by the Higginson Book Company, is possibly the most haunted building in Salem. Though Corwin's ghost, per se, hasn't been seen in the house, he's certainly a likely candidate. Stories abound of candles being melted, shaped, and moved around; garbage cans being flipped upside down; alarms being set off by unknown sources; books, desks, and lamps being tossed around helter-skelter; and a persistent cold spot that fills an entire corner room. One of the most famous paranormal incidents occurred when a Polaroid photograph was taken that captured, quite unexpectedly, an apparition of a very spooky-looking woman, with matted and tousled black hair and a long black gown, who placed herself squarely between the photographer and his subject. She was the archetypal witch of centuries past, if ever there was one.

Another remarkable incident happened when a document that was about to be fetched from the closet came drifting out unassisted by human hands, unrolled itself, and laid itself out neatly before the eyes of two speechless men. Maybe the loathsome Corwin has turned over a new, more promising leaf, with the stinging realization that his radical, puritanical conduct was not the ticket to Heaven after all, and he'd best be changing his ways if he ever wanted to see the Light. Or maybe the witch in the Polaroid snapshot finally caught up with him and cast a "nice" spell on him. Let's hope it lasts an eternity.

Dogtown: The Lost Village

At one time, Dogtown Commons had a population of about a hundred people—not bad for one of the earliest settlements in our country. That was in 1692. Today all that remains is a wooded, rocky plateau with an occasional part of a foundation, such as stone steps or broken stone walls, buried beneath the dense brush. This was once a thriving little community whose inhabitants lived off the land and by their wits—or, I should say, by their varied magical gifts. Many of the inhabitants at one time were witches, so the ghost town is sometimes called the "Village of the Lost Witches" or the "Village of a Hundred Witches." It has also been referred to as a "village lost in time," and indeed it is. All are appropriate names. But how did it get its official name of Dogtown?

When Dogtown was first settled, it consisted of a hardy bunch of colonists who preferred the safety of the rugged, boulder-laden terrain to the adjacent pirate-infested shoreline of Gloucester and Cape Ann. However, as soon as "the coast was clear," so to speak, and the pirating British had left the area, the original families of Dogtown moved to the more promising communities they'd previously avoided. The only remaining inhabitants were widows who refused to leave the homes they'd built with their loved ones. But their husbands were lost to the sea, and without adequate manpower to protect the women and children, they found themselves in a very vulnerable position, so they armed themselves with guard dogs. The years went by, and the few remaining residents of the settlement succumbed to old age. When the last person finally passed on, all that remained were empty houses and dogs that roamed wild—hence the name Dogtown.

Dogtown was vacant for only a short time before the local lunatics, hobos, and crones realized they'd hit the jackpot and stumbled upon a whole neighborhood of free turnkey homes. They were a colorful bunch all right, and when the witches and warlocks came to town, the new inhabitants had no problem sharing the remaining homes with them. The personalities that came out of the last batch of townspeople to inhabit Dogtown in the late 1700s and early 1800s were unparalleled, and many of the residents' names deservedly went down in history: the snobbish healer and fortune-teller Easter Carter; self-proclaimed wizard John Woodman; Old Ruth, a freed slave who dressed and worked like a man; the formidable broomstick-riding witch Margaret Wesson; and the generous Becky Rich, whose remedy of natural herbs and leaves was a sure cure for any ailment. There was also a wannabe dentist—and God help the woeful patient who sought treatment from him, for he actually was a sea captain by trade. Another fellow made a living plying his services of door-to-door ironing and knitting. A couple of younger witches found that prostituting bewitched young sailors was a lucrative venture. The most feared of all the Dogtown witches was Tammy Younger, a large woman who could stop passersby with the evil eye, freezing them in their tracks, and then summoned their belongings to drift through the air right to her feet. That's what they said, anyway.

The last of the Dogtowners was Black Neil Finson, a hobo and friend of the witches, who died in 1814. He was found alone, half starved and frozen, digging and clawing in the dirt beneath the house of the prostitute witches, believing until his dying day that the profits they made were buried in their cellar. He must have thought highly of them, because he believed their wealth was substantial. After being removed from their house by a local official from Rockport, Finson was sent to the town's poorhouse, where he died shortly after.

As if the rich history of Dogtown's populace weren't interesting enough, in the late 1800s, things got even more peculiar, when a philanthropist named Roger Babson hired stone carvers to carve "good" words and phrases into the boulders that adorn Dogtown's land. It was a nonsensical request, because the land was practically barren at the time, and nobody—save the occasional visitor—would even see them. The words carved into the stones include "Use Your Head," "Help Your Mother," and "Study." Good old puritanical advice, perhaps to cleanse the environment of its former, wilder days. But the past will always linger there.

Visitors determined enough to follow the footpath to Dogtown are rewarded with a sense of peacefulness as their eyes focus on the etched words memorialized by Babson. What better place to meditate than among the lonely trees, within earshot of the ocean, perched on a boulder bearing a simple spiritual message? The only thing that might break the self-induced trance is the distant scream of a phantom lunatic or the muted shout of an angry fortune-teller of yesteryear. Such haunting sounds are still reported from visitors to Dogtown, where the past stirs only occasionally before settling back down to a reverent calm.

Rockport's Witch Wesson

Everyone knew not to invade Margaret Wesson's space. You don't mess with "old Meg," they'd say. Why, the crazy old bat was said to fly her broom over the New England coastline and cast the "evil eye" at whim. Meg lived in Rockport, near the other popular "witching" grounds called Dogtown Commons, until her death by mysterious gunshot wounds—from a gun that was fired five hundred miles away!

Two soldiers from Gloucester were at camp in Nova Scotia during the siege of Louisburg in 1745, when they became annoyed by a crow that seemed to be taunting them, cawing angrily and fluttering about their heads. They tried shooting at it and throwing stones, but nothing deterred the determined bird. It had no intention of ending the harassment—clearly, it meant business.

Finally, it occurred to the men that the bird had to be a witch—and not just any witch. It had to be Witch Wesson, the woman from Rockport whom they'd foolishly offended in a heated argument before leaving town—the woman who promised she'd teach them a lesson, even if it was the last thing she did. Realizing that their luck had run out and old Meg had finally caught up with them, they cut two silver buttons from their uniforms—pure silver being the preferred antidote for the evils of witchcraft. They loaded the buttons into their guns and took aim at the crow. With the first shot, the crow's leg was broken, and with the second, it fell dead.

When the soldiers returned to Rockport, they learned that Meg had fallen with an injured leg at the very moment they fired on the crow, and she died shortly thereafter. Upon examination of her body, the same buttons the men had used to take down the bird were found in the old woman's flesh.

Dungeon Rock

Hiram Marble was a man who spent his entire life—and squandered away his life savings—seeking the treasure alleged to be buried at Dungeon Rock in the Lynn Woods Memorial Park. He claimed that the spirit of seventeenth-century pirate Thomas Veal had contacted him from beyond the grave—which, in this case, was actually the cave in which Veal had been entombed during an earthquake in 1658—and told him where to find his treasure, so he purchased the property and began digging. It was to no avail. Like many treasure hunters before him, Marble's tireless efforts proved futile. When the determined man died in 1868, his son carried on the family's obsessive quest for the buried treasure, until he too died in 1880. The Marble family is buried just a short distance from the place that consumed their lives and ultimately left them destitute. Some believe Hiram and his son may still be laboring in the cave, as single-minded in death as they were in life. If they aren't the ones haunting it, perhaps it's Veal himself, stubbornly refusing to let go of his material possessions, even though they are of no use to him now.

The tunnel at Dungeon Rock is open only during the day; an iron door seals the entrance at night. Many people have reported taking daytime photographs of orbs and other types of spirit energy while in the cave. Others have heard moaning, crying, and growling that can't be explained, and some have even had success capturing spirit voices on tape. The sense of being watched and the feeling of cold chills have been enough to send more than a few people running from the cave. There's really no doubt that the cave is haunted. The only question is, by whom? And, of course, whether there really is buried treasure at Dungeon Rock.

The Gentle Son

According to author Charles Skinner, Jacob Hurd lived in Ipswich with his wife and meek son in the late 1600s. He was as fearful of witches as most others caught up in the witch hysteria and was suspicious of anyone who didn't conform to what he considered normal behavior. This posed a problem, for his own son seemed to dance to the beat of a different drummer. The boy had no interest in farming or learning an honorable trade. Very much the introvert, he kept to himself, walking alone and talking to the birds. He was happy just to make up rhymes, pick flowers, and dream his days away.

One day he decided to share a vision he'd had with his parents. He told them he had seen a "golden horse with a tail and mane of silver, on which he had ridden over land and sea, climbing mountains and swimming rivers." His father was mortified, thinking his son was certainly bewitched, and he yelled at him, "Thou knowest thou art lying!" With that, he struck the child. The boy staggered into his mother's arms, and by twisted coincidence, he fell very ill that night. In a feverish state, he raved about his horse and the places he would see. His guilt-ridden father sat by him, too torn up inside to speak, and never left the boy's side. Just before the youngster closed his eyes for the last time, he looked at his father and said he heard his horse "pawing in the road," and his father could have sworn he actually saw it there, too. Then, with a peaceful smile on his face, the child slumped into his pillow, lifeless.

Some time later, Hurd set out early to see three witches hanged, unaware that his own death day had arrived as well. His body was soon discovered by the roadside, with an Indian arrow through his heart and an ax in his head. That night, his horse came flying down the road spattered with blood and foam. Hurd's grieving wife ran to the door, horrified. But the bloodied horse changed before her eyes. Its sides suddenly shone like gold in the sunlight, and its mane and tail were a glittery silver. Instead of crying out as the horse passed by, she caught her breath—for there before her very eyes was her dearly beloved son, riding on horseback. His face was lit in a heavenly glow, and he threw a kiss at her. Her little poet lived on in spirit where all his dreams finally came true.

Greater Boston

THE GREATER BOSTON AREA IS BOUNDED TO THE WEST BY WORCESTER County and to the east by the North and South Shores. Vertically, it stretches from New Hampshire to Rhode Island, so it actually covers a lot of ground. Boston is not only the state capital, but also the largest—and oldest—city in all of New England. As such, you'll often hear "first" and "oldest" used in conjunction with "in America" in researching places of historic significance in the Boston area (for example, Harvard is the oldest university in America). This cosmopolitan area is also a melting pot of ethnic cultures . . . and it's apparently a melting pot of supernatural phenomena as well. The capital region boasts of UFO sightings—including, of course, the first in the country—haunted inns and hotels, Virgin Mary apparitions, a nineteenth-century resurrection, and the illustrious Dover Demon, a cryptozoological enigma.

UFOs North of Boston

The Greater Merrimack Valley and the area north of Boston are definitely hot spots in the state for UFO sightings. Why this is, no one knows, but the fact is that Essex and Middlesex Counties alone have had roughly three-fourths the number of *reported* sightings in the entire state (many cases go unreported for fear of ridicule).

Though the Massachusetts branch of the Mutual UFO Network (MUFON) believes that a solid 90 percent of what were originally thought to be UFOs in the Bay State have had logical explanations, roughly eighty sightings still defy explanation.

According to the historical files of Massachusetts MUFON online, the first reported sighting in the area was in 1846, when a "big luminous flying disc" released over Lowell a "fetid-smelling jelly" that weighed 442 pounds. Luckily, it didn't land on anyone. Details are scarce on that account. In 1960, a husband and wife watched a pulsating sphere of red and white lights in the skies over Bedford for five minutes before it disappeared. An individual in Woburn followed a color-changing streak of light across the sky for several seconds in 1961, and several days later, a North Wilmington woman reported a "bright, white sphere" the size of a grapefruit moving easterly across the sky.

In 1962, a man working on the roof of a house in Woburn was fortunate enough to have time to grab his Polaroid camera and take pictures of the UFO he watched for nearly a full minute. Only one picture revealed a circular object with an unusual marking in its center. Photographs were also obtained from a sighting in Burlington that year. In 1963, Burlington's Richard Hall was quoted in *The UFO Evidence* as saying, "An unidentified white light was observed descending, changing color; finally appearing silvery. The UFO then circled the area, disappearing behind objects on the visible horizon." And in 1966, two residents of Chelmsford watched as a UFO flew overhead at about 9:05 P.M. It had "two extremely bright red lights with a string of dim bluish white lights in between them. No structure could be seen, but the lights moved in a way that suggested they were attached to an unseen object."

In the North Shore region, two well-publicized and documented cases occurred in 1952 and 1966. The first occurred when a seaman at the Salem Coast Guard Station saw four bright lights in the sky. Just as a guardsman arrived in response to the seaman's frantic calls, the lights dimmed, then brightened quickly, and the seaman had time to take one photograph through the screened office window before the lights vanished altogether. That one spectacular photograph was subsequently published by many forms of media. In 1962, after years of trying to come up with an explanation for the mysterious lights the seaman had observed, the U.S. Coast

Guard wrote, "It has never been determined what caused the phenomenal lights."

The 1966 case involved nine witnesses in Beverly. It began when an eleven-year-old girl looked out of her bedroom window and saw a bright, blinking object the size of a car, with flashing blue, green, red, and white lights. It was shaped like a football and made a whizzing sound as it passed over neighborhood rooftops. When it landed in a field behind the local high school, the girl raced downstairs to tell her father what she'd seen. Her father told her to go back to bed, and he went back to trying to get the TV working again—the screen had just gone blank. Two of her mother's friends who happened to walk in at that very moment offered to go to the field and investigate, because they, too, could see the flashing lights from where they were and assumed it was just a plane. They were wrong.

Joined by the girl's mother, the three women ventured over to the high school field and were stunned by what they saw. There were actually three UFOs. Two were off in the distance, but the one that was closer was just as the girl had described. When the strange object shifted direction and started coming toward the women, they began to run. One of them was paralyzed to the spot when the object hovered directly overhead. She got a much closer look than she would have liked, but at least she was able to give a very clear description later. She was pulled out of her hypnotic state when her friends called to her, and she ran to join them.

By the time they got back to their apartment building, the object was drifting over the school building, and other neighbors were stepping outside to witness the strange object. The police thought they were receiving prank calls at first, but they soon stood corrected. They raced toward the school in their police cars and got close enough to confirm that the object was definitely not an airplane or a helicopter; but just as they arrived at the school grounds, the object flew off, picking up speed as it went along.

This case was unique in that so many witnesses, including officers of the law, gave the same vivid account of what they saw. All their stories matched. The object lingered much longer than the typical reported sightings of UFOs, so more people were able to observe it. The sighting was so credible that it has been used as a sort of UFO "poster child." It was thoroughly investigated by the

National Investigations Committee on Aerial Phenomena (NICAP) and the Condon Committee, a group that studies UFOs for government agencies. It's unusual for sightings to get very far before being dismissed, but the Beverly sighting went all the way to the top.

A final report issued by the Condon Committee to the U.S. Air Force said, "While the current cases investigated did not yield impressive residual evidence, even in the narrative content, to support a hypothesis that an alien vehicle was physically present, narratives of past events, such as the 1966 incident at Beverly, Mass., would fit no other explanation if the testimony of the witnesses is taken at full value."

Northern Massachusetts and the Greater Merrimack Valley certainly seem to have been intergalactic stops several decades ago, though UFO sightings have declined markedly in recent years. Maybe the cost of saucer fuel got to be out of this world. It seems to be a universal problem.

The Colonial Inn

The original section of the Colonial Inn at 48 Monument Square in Concord was built in 1716 by a physician and soldier, Captain John Minot. Two nineteenth-century buildings were added to the Minot house in the late 1800s, and another sizable addition was added in the 1960s and 1970s. Not surprisingly, it was during that most recent renovation period that a bedside ghost first appeared, as ghosts often do during reconstruction of their former romping grounds.

A newlywed couple was given Room 24 on the second floor in 1966. The large, lovely room is in the old part of the building (the Minot house) and overlooks historic Monument Square. Though she didn't mention it to the innkeeper at the time of her departure, the young bride sent a letter to the inn several weeks after their visit, describing an interesting encounter she'd had during her stay:

> I have always prided myself on being a fairly sane individual, but on the night of June 14, I began to have my doubts. On that night, I saw a ghost in your inn. The next morning, I felt too foolish to mention it to the management, so my husband and I continued on our honeymoon. I wondered whether or not any sightings of a ghost had been reported, or if any history of one was involved in the history of the inn.

The incident sounds very melodramatic. I was awakened in the middle of the night by a presence in the room—a feeling that some unknown being was in the midst. As I opened my eyes, I saw a grayish figure at the side of my bed, to the left, about four feet away. It was not a distinct person, but a shadowy mass in the shape of a standing figure. It remained still for a moment then slowly floated to the foot of the bed, in front of the fireplace. After pausing a few seconds, the apparition slowly melted away. It was a terrifying experience. I was so frightened I could not scream. I was frozen to the spot. . . .

For the remainder of the night, I could not fall asleep. It was spent trying to conjure a logical explanation for the apparition. It was not a reflection of the moon, as all the curtains were completely closed. Upon relating the incident to my husband, he said the ghost was included in the price of the room.

The innkeeper responded to the letter with a polite and jovial reply, suggesting that perhaps the ghost was that of one of the many famous people who had stayed at the inn in the last couple hundred years (including Ralph Waldo Emerson and Franklin D. Roosevelt) or perhaps it was Doc Minot, still making his bedside rounds. Another possibility was Henry David Thoreau, whose family lived in the original Minot home.

Today Jurgen Demisch is the lucky proprietor. According to the inn's website, www.concordscolonialinn.com, if you'd like a haunted room at the inn, just ask for Room 24. As far as they know, "the other rooms are ghost-free."

The Stormbreeder

Peter Rugg lived on Middle Street in Boston with his wife and young daughter. There was nothing outstanding about the man, except his occasional temper tantrums. He was famous for his sudden, unpredictable outbursts, and his family and friends were sure it would get him in trouble one day. That inevitable day came in the fall of 1770. Rugg and his young daughter, his faithful little sidekick, visited Concord by horse and carriage. After Rugg had taken care of business, they stopped at a tavern owned by Rugg's longtime friend for a drink before heading back toward Boston. The skies soon turned dark gray, and the wind picked up. A violent thunderstorm was approaching, and the tavern owner insisted that Rugg and his daughter stay the night rather than risk the trip home in such inclement weather. But *nobody* should insist that Rugg do anything—not if they knew the man. Rugg's defiant words to the innkeeper as he hoisted his daughter onto the rain-drenched carriage seat became a self-fulfilling prophecy: "Let the storm increase! I will see home tonight in spite of it, or may I never see home!" With that he was off, never to be seen in his mortal form again.

Several nights later, while Rugg's neighbors were searching by lantern light for the man and child, heavy hooves were heard fast approaching the lane on which Rugg lived. They heard Rugg order his large, black horse to stop as he looked toward his house, but the beast never slowed. Witnesses said the man at the reins looked wet and weary, and the soaking child at his side clung desperately to his arm. As the apparition passed, the rain fell more heavily. In fact, sightings of Rugg's ghost—and there were many—were followed by violent thunderstorms so often that he became known as "the Stormbreeder." Apparitions of a man and child in their swift, horse-driven carriage were reported for nearly 150 years from as far away as Hartford, Connecticut; Providence, Rhode Island; and the New Hampshire hills. Always the ghostly ensemble was surrounded by a strange purplish glow, and always the distraught father and child appeared dazed and desperate.

One man from Connecticut said Rugg spoke to him before vanishing into thin air. He said, "I have lost the road to Boston. My name is Peter Rugg." Indeed, he was way off course. But he hasn't been seen in a very long time now. One can only hope that he and his daughter finally found their way to the Other Side, where his wife, who died of a broken heart within a year of their disappearance, was waiting with open arms.

Boston Light and the Ghost Walk

Boston Light is the oldest lighthouse in America, originally built in 1716 on Little Brewster Island at the entrance of Boston Harbor. It's no surprise that a number of legends are associated with such a historic landmark. After all, it has borne witness to countless shipwrecks near the island as well as the drownings of its first two keepers shortly after taking their assignments. Many believe that Boston

Light is haunted—and with good reason. Apparitions have been seen drifting through the lantern room, feline mascots hiss at unseen presences, unexplained footsteps are sometimes heard, and cold spots have been widely reported.

Several miles east of Little Brewster Island, there's a peculiar area of the ocean that locals call the "Ghost Walk." Here there seems to be some sort of atmospheric anomaly that prevents sound from entering the area. Even the enormous bell from Boston Light cannot be heard in the Ghost Walk. The phenomena received so much hype in the late 1800s that a team of students from the Massachusetts Institute of Technology was dispatched to Little Brewster Island for an entire summer to experiment with foghorn signals in an attempt to reach the area in question. No signal—not even with the largest horn or siren—was able to penetrate the mysterious sound barrier. It remains unexplained to this day.

The Dover Demon

What has big orange eyes, a disproportionately large head and extremities, and a frail, spindly body? Answer: a famous cryptozoological critter known as the "Dover Demon," the Boston area's most famous paranormal entity. To this day, nobody knows who or what it was, or where it came from, but its encounters with three Dover residents in 1977 quickly propelled it to legendary status.

The name Dover Demon is somewhat of a misnomer, because this being never showed any propensity whatsoever toward evil of any kind. Quite the contrary. It was described as being "frozen like a deer in headlights," "scurrying away toward a gully," "sitting on its hind end by the side of the road," and "creeping skittishly along the stone wall." Hardly like any demon I've ever heard of. But Dover Demon does have a nice, catchy ring to it, and it's obviously more memorable than, say, the Dover Deer.

The first encounter with the so-called demon occurred on April 21, 1977, at 10:30 P.M. Bill Bartlett was driving down Farm Street with two of his seventeen-year-old friends when he spotted a small creature creeping along a wall of stones. It stopped and looked right into the car's headlights with large eyes that looked "like two orange marbles." Bartlett didn't slow the vehicle for a better look—probably because his mind was so focused on trying to digest what it had just seen that it couldn't process any more instructions—but when Bartlett told his friends he had just seen something bizarre, they persuaded him to turn around and go back. (The other two had been engaged in deep conversation and hadn't noticed the creature.) Unfortunately, the little whatchamacallit was gone when they returned. The shaken young man dropped his friends off and went home to draw a picture of what he had seen—a picture that would be circulated and reproduced worldwide over the years since his encounter. The creature's head was the size and shape of a watermelon and had no discernible features, except the prominent glowing eyes. The body was disproportionately small, compared to the head and extremities. The four-foot-tall being was naked, and its skin appeared rough in texture. It crept along the wall like a monkey, in an upright stance alternating with walking on all fours.

A couple hours after Bartlett's sighting, in the wee hours of April 22, a fifteen-year-old boy was walking home from his girlfriend's house and was at the intersection of Miller Hill Road and Farm Street when he saw a small figure approaching him that looked human. He called out to it, thinking it might be a particular friend, because he couldn't think of anyone else who would be walking along that quiet stretch of road at such a late hour, but it didn't answer. It just stopped where it was and stared back at him, as if sizing him up. When the boy took his next step toward it, the skittish little creature dashed to a gully nearby. The boy followed boldly from a distance and found the wee fellow hugging a tree on the other side of the brook, where he was able to get a better view of it. But his courage was short-lived. He didn't know what the thing's intention was. Would it pounce across the brook at him? He didn't have to ask himself twice. With a sudden turn, he raced back to the road and hitched a ride the rest of the way home. His description matched Bartlett's to a tee, even though the two had not known of each other's experiences.

But Bartlett did tell his friend Will Taintor about the incident. The next night, Taintor was driving a friend home when the girl claimed to see a small, apelike creature in the car's headlights on Springdale Avenue. She allegedly knew nothing about Bartlett and Taintor's conversation regarding the mysterious being, but her report matched the earlier sightings, with the exception of eye color.

She swore that what she saw had green luminous eyes, whereas the young men had seen orange eyes—a minor detail, considering all of the other similarities among the three stories. But that would be the last time the Dover Demon was ever seen.

Paranormal investigators quickly converged on the area. It's not every day that an exotic new creature is discovered. They found the witnesses all to be credible citizens with no reason to have fabricated their stories. In fact, the three youths were press-shy and had told only family and friends about their disturbing encounters. The investigators ruled out several theories posed by the more skeptical local residents. It definitely wasn't a goat or a colt or a newborn moose, as some had suggested. But it *did* apparently meet the criteria for a cryptozoological being, because no respectable source on cryptozoology would even think of leaving the Dover Demon out today. We may never find out what it was, but that's okay. My mother once said that it's always better to leave something to the imagination.

The Omni Parker House

Located in the heart of downtown Boston, across from Boston Common, is America's longest continuously operated hotel, the four-diamond Omni Parker House, which opened in 1855. The hotel's founder is Harvey Parker. The illustrious Mr. Parker arrived in Boston in 1826 with nothing but a pocket full of change, a penchant for hard work, and lofty entrepreneurial dreams of the restaurateur kind. He went to work immediately as a coachman for an affluent socialite, biding his time until opportunity knocked. Then one of his favorite pubs went up for sale, and he bought it. Under his brilliant management, the restaurant became one of the most popular in the city—so popular that he decided to expand his business by adding a luxury hotel in which his diners could stay after their fine meals. It was called the Parker House until the 1990s, when the Omni hotel chain purchased it and officially changed the name to the Omni Parker House.

The hotel was the official meeting place of the exclusive Saturday Club, which included the likes of Henry Wadsworth Longfellow, Charles Dickens, Ralph Waldo Emerson, and Henry David

Thoreau. Oliver Wendell Holmes wrote a famous poem called "At the Saturday Club," which made reference to the famous ghost or ghosts that haunt the hotel. One stanza says, "Such guests! What famous names its record boasts, whose owners wander in the mob of ghosts." The famous guests have included nearly every president since Ulysses S. Grant, as well as John Wilkes Booth (said to have plotted his assassination of Lincoln while staying at the hotel), Judy Garland, Babe Ruth, and Madonna, to name just a few. The gentlemanly ghost of owner Harvey Parker has appeared at the foot of the bed of more than one surprised guest, asking if they had everything they required. (At that point, I would have asked for a stiff drink!) Others claim to have seen Parker's ghost wandering the halls, especially on the tenth floor, which wasn't even there during his lifetime. The apparition has been described as a bearded man dressed in Victorian-era clothing; he appears solid for only a moment before fading away.

On both the ninth and tenth floors, people have reported seeing orbs of white light and hearing inexplicable sounds. The third floor is the other "active" floor, in the paranormal sense. One of the elevators stops at the third floor without anyone calling for it or pressing the third-floor button. In the past, it happened so frequently that engineers were called in to inspect the elevator thoroughly, but they could find nothing wrong with it. Some believe that it's the ghost of actress Charlotte Cushman, who stayed frequently in the Dickens Suite of the hotel, where she had been living. Maybe she still hasn't left her favorite place. Or maybe someone else is haunting the Omni's elevators.

Room 303 was turned into a storage closet when it became apparent that it was very haunted. A traveling liquor salesman died in that room years ago, and some believe he's responsible for the taunting laughter heard and the smell of whiskey that pervaded the room before it was finally renovated. Staff members and guests alike have seen ominous shadows on the walls and found bathroom fixtures operating with no apparent assistance. But what would you expect in a place that has hosted, for 150 years, thousands of famous celebrities and historic visitors? It only adds to the atmosphere of authenticity—rubbing shoulders with the rich and famous of the past in a posh, genuine Victorian hotel.

Charlesgate Hall

I've written a lot of true ghost stories, four volumes' worth, in fact, but I have to admit that this was the most disturbing—to the point that I wasn't even sure I wanted to write it. I think it's because of my inexplicable aversion to Ouija boards, which play a significant role in the haunted happenings at 4 Charlesgate, just off Beacon Street in Boston's Back Bay area. From the 1970s to the early 1990s, Ouija boards spawned so many evil and unnatural events at the old Charlesgate Hall dormitory that Emerson College officials prohibited possession of the controversial board on college property. Ironically, those students who bucked authority and tempted fate soon discovered that the very boards they were told not to possess were actually trying to possess them!

J. Pickering Putnam designed and built the opulent Charlesgate Hotel in 1891 and lived there until his death in 1917. The hotel was popular among Boston society's elite circle right up through 1947, when it was sold to Boston University and turned into a student housing complex. That was when things started getting a little weird, but it was still the calm before the storm.

Under Boston University's ownership, the sixth floor was found to be very haunted. An alarm clock went off repeatedly at the same time each morning in a room where a suicide had occurred, even though it was not even set to go off at that time. In another room, students found that they were unable to open one of the closet doors. All three of the students assigned to that room felt resistance turning the doorknob and an inexplicable anxiety about opening the door, but it wasn't until later that they learned a former student had hanged herself in that very closet. A different room was boarded up after a resident advisor ran into the room of a screaming student and found the horrified freshman lying in bed with an apparition suspended directly over him.

Boston University sold the building in 1972, and for the next nine years, the rooms were rented out to just about anyone—students, working adults, and even allegedly a group of devil worshipers who were seen practicing black magic through the cracks in their doors. By that time, supernatural events were increasing and becoming more intense. Many people believe the invasion of evil forces occurred during those reckless years.

When Emerson College purchased Charlesgate Hall in 1981, it was renovated to the tune of $1 million before a new wave of students was allowed to move in. Paranormal researchers agree that the number of prepubescent and adolescent people in a haunted location directly correlates to the volume and intensity of paranormal happenings. There seems to be something about the vitality and life force of that age group that attracts energy-guzzling entities like moths to an open flame. Suddenly Charlesgate Hall came alive again—with both the seen and the unseen.

Emerson College archivist Robert Fleming encouraged the hall's residents to share their stories for the college archives. He could never have predicted the sheer volume of stories that came pouring in. One young woman told him that one night her roommate was replaced by a phantom roommate. The girl awoke when she felt someone climbing up from the lower bunk she slept on to the top bunk, as her roommate typically did. Then she heard her getting comfortable and settling in, so she turned on the light to ask her friend why she had come back early, but nobody was there! The girl left the room and slept elsewhere that night. When she returned in the morning, she found that the sheets and blankets on the top bunk were pulled back and rumpled, as if someone had actually slept there—but her roommate always made her bed before she left.

Other students' experiences were clearly sparked by the use of Ouija boards. Messages that came through the popular, but controversial, divining board were unusually threatening. Students were exposing themselves to evil entities that were quick to take advantage of the open invitation put forth by use of the board. In one such case, an entity with a grudge against a particular male student spelled out its hatred by repeating the young man's name obsessively and even saying the student "had to die." Several nights later, the student went to take a shower while his roommates foolishly continued to play with the board. When he noticed that the light in the bathroom was flickering, he reached up and screwed the bulb in tighter, fixing the problem. Then he stepped into the shower and was all soaped up when the lightbulb again started flickering. Unbeknownst to him, his friends had, at that very moment, received a message from the evil spirit that simply spelled out "H-A-H-A." They asked what was so funny, and it spelled out "A-C-D-C." Meanwhile, back in the bathroom, the male student thoughtlessly stepped out of the shower to tighten the bulb again, when he stopped short of doing it with a sickening realization: He was standing in a pool of water and would have been electrocuted. So he dried off and went out to his buddies, looking pale and nauseated. He told them what had just about happened, and they told him who had caused it. The evil spirit had actually tried to kill him!

There were many more stories just as disturbing from other students, but everything came to a grinding halt when Emerson College sold Charlesgate Hall to a private developer, who has since turned the spirit-infested building into spirit-free condominiums. When the students left, the evil spirits left, thank God. And that was the end of that.

North America's First UFO

"Row, row, row your boat, gently down the stream. Merrily, merrily, merrily, merrily, life is but a dream." That childhood nursery rhyme could well have been written by the three men who spotted the first UFO in North America while drifting down the Muddy River in Boston in 1638. It had to have been a surreal experience for the Pilgrims, who had never even heard of UFOs, especially when they realized they had experienced the "lost-time" phenomenon, with which today's UFO researchers are so familiar.

James Everell and two friends were rowing merrily down the river one night when a large, bright light appeared suddenly in the sky directly over them. The square, fiery object "contracted into the figure of a swine" before moving "swift as an arrow" toward Charleston, according to the men. They watched, stunned, as the light moved back and forth between Boston and Charleston for what seemed like several hours. When it finally disappeared, the men realized that they had somehow ended up about a mile *up* the river from where they had originally put their boat in. They had been mysteriously transported against the current, with no memory of having rowed back upstream themselves, which would have required some conscious effort on their part. It was simply impossible.

Had it not been for the credibility of the three gentlemen, described as sober and discreet, as well as another individual who claimed to have seen a similar object on the river at about the same time, the story may have gone no further. Instead, John Winthrop, governor of the Massachusetts Bay Colony, wrote of the incident in his book, *The History of New England, 1630–1639,* so it went down in history as the first documented report of a UFO sighting in North America.

Central Burying Ground

There's more to Boston Common's Central Burying Ground on the South Side than what meets the eye, and I'm not just talking about the spirits that most certainly inhabit the land. You would never know that the dead are buried far beyond the scope of the area designated as the Central Burying Ground. In fact, nearly all of the common's forty-eight acres hold corpses from Colonial times, when the undesirables of society were executed and buried there with no stones to mark their remains.

That may be why it's so hard to identify the little girl who tried to befriend Dr. Matt Rutger in the 1970s, while the good dentist was visiting the cemetery. He later said that he felt someone tap his shoulder several times, and then he felt a tug on his collar from behind. Clearly, someone wanted his attention. But he was alone . . . or so he thought. At that moment, his awareness was drawn to the rear corner of the cemetery, where he saw something move out of the corner of his eye. It was a young girl wearing a soiled, oversized white dress. Long auburn hair framed her gaunt, ashen face, and something about her just wasn't right—or real. The dentist turned to run toward the front gate, but he stopped in his tracks when he realized that the source of his fear had suddenly appeared at the front gate, where she stood staring solemnly at him. For several minutes, he watched the young spirit relocate instantly to various areas of the cemetery, as if showing off an impressive, newfound ability.

Overcoming his initial apprehension, the dentist took a daring step toward the child. That was when he confirmed what he had already begun to suspect. She wasn't solid. The closer he got, the more she faded, until she had finally disappeared altogether. As the dentist continued on his way to his car, he reached into his pocket for his keys. That's when he felt a small, icy hand next to his own, and he watched dumbfounded as his keys drifted up into the air, hovered momentarily, and then dropped to the ground. It was his last interaction with the young girl—but it was more than enough to turn a nonbeliever into a believer!

Resurrection

Ephraim Gray was an eccentric recluse who lived in a suburb of Malden in the mid-1800s, along with his faithful companion, a servant who kept Ephraim's house . . . and his secrets. Though Ephraim was rarely seen on the street, he was often smelled—that is, a strong, chemical-like odor often drifted from his house onto the street, causing passersby to wonder aloud what he was doing in there. They could see his silhouette through the shades in the upstairs window, but nobody could discern what covert activities the old hermit was up to, and his servant was sworn to secrecy.

The townspeople were left with inquiring minds for years, but the truth was finally revealed one day in 1850, when Ephraim's servant walked into the police department and reported that his friend and employer had died by natural means during the night. The loyal servant then told the local mortician that Ephraim's body was not to be tampered with in any way, except to place it into his crypt in the Malden Cemetery. He went on to explain that Gray—a self-taught chemist—had been working on a secret chemical concoction that would halt aging and ensure his immortality. He hadn't perfected the elixir at the time of his death, but he had taken enough of the substance over the years to at least ensure that his corpse would remain unaffected by the natural decay process. Besides, the servant was the soul heir to Ephraim's estate, but only on the condition that he made sure Ephraim's body went straight from his home to his tomb, with no stops in between for the usual preparation and disposal of corpses. His wishes were granted. No recipe for the secret elixir was ever found in the home the men shared, even after the servant passed away several years later. Both apparently took the secret formula—if there truly was one—to their graves. But Ephraim may have managed to put the finishing touches on his potion from the Great Beyond, because somehow, as the legend goes, he rose (or was taken) from the grave between 1850 and the early 1900s.

A young man from Malden told a group of curious Harvard students of Ephraim Gray's strange experiment, and they couldn't resist visiting his grave twenty years after Gray was buried to see if his body had indeed avoided decay. Imagine their surprise when they pried open the casket and found the body in not just good, but *perfect* condition, completely unaffected by the years. It looked as if he were still alive. Their curiosity satisfied, they quickly sealed the casket back up securely, or so they later claimed, and agreed to tell nobody of their findings, because if their grave-tampering activities were ever discovered, they would be kicked out of medical school, or worse. Luckily for them, their secret was safe until many years later, when they had all become successful, middle-aged physicians.

In the early twentieth century, the highway department needed to move Malden Cemetery to a new location to make way for a road that would go straight through the burial ground. When they got to Gray's crypt, they found his coffin to be unusually light, so they opened it up and discovered that it was completely empty. That was when word leaked out about the young medical students' visit to the crypt, but all of the men involved vehemently insisted they had not removed the body and had, in fact, resealed the coffin with the utmost care.

Nobody has ever figured out how Gray's body got out of his tomb. Had he perfected his potion on the Other Side and actually returned to life—a modern-day resurrection? If so, does he still walk among us mere mortals, never to age or die? Or, perhaps more plausibly, was his body carefully removed, studied, and disposed of, in the name of science and medicine? We may never know. Ephraim Gray's life and death remain shrouded in mystery.

Stone's Public House

Matt Murphy is the owner and chef of one of Ashland's most popular pubs and restaurants, Stone's Public House at 179 Main Street. The restaurant, formerly an inn, is known for its friendly atmosphere, its excellent cuisine—and its ghosts. A myriad of paranormal experiences have plagued the staff and patrons over the years. It's pure speculation as to who really is haunting the inn, but the mounting psychic impressions bring several individuals into play. There's John Stone himself, the farmer-turned-entrepreneur who built the place in 1834; a friendly young girl who hangs out in the kitchen; a female member of the staff who died there many years ago; and a gambler who allegedly was killed accidentally and buried in the basement (not accidentally).

The stern-faced Captain John Stone originally built the place as a hotel called the Railroad House when he learned that a railroad would be running through his property, but he ran the business for only two years. Since then, scores of innkeepers and thousands of patrons have passed through its doors, each adding his or her own little piece of history to the entire life story of the building—and some of that history was sadly quite tragic. A previous owner was struck down in his prime by a train when he attempted to push a stranded motorist off the Boston and Albany Railroad track adjacent to the property. Many years before that, a niece of one of the former employees allegedly died while being cared for on the premises, and a barmaid supposedly died while working there many years ago. According to one psychic, a gambler from New York was accused of cheating at a game of poker by Captain Stone himself, and when he became outraged and difficult, Stone allegedly struck him on the head with the end of a gun, intending only to subdue the man. But the story goes that the man died from the blow and was buried in the basement to conceal the crime. No body has ever been unearthed, however, and it's not for lack of trying.

These unfortunate situations may help explain some of the paranormal incidents. The murdered gambler, if he existed, certainly has every right to hold a grudge. He could conceivably be responsible for making glass ashtrays shatter for no reason and for sending jars that were set far back on the shelves crashing to the floor. And if Stone was a man of temper, as many believe, was he responsible for putting the chokehold on one unlucky female patron? Or was it the equally irritable gambler? The poor lady could barely call for her bill and was too polite to leave without paying.

There's also a little girl whose spirit has been seen in the kitchen early in the morning. Employees say she looked to be about nine or ten and smiled shyly before fading away. One morning, they arrived to find the kitchen window broken from the inside—glass was on the outside, as if someone had pushed through the window. But nobody had been inside during the night. Then there's the matter of an old, blood-stained girl's dress that was found in the attic. The dress itself seems to be haunted, because one employee removed it from the building to show someone, and frightening things happened to her the whole time she had it in the trunk of her car. She passed it off to her boyfriend, thinking it might just be her imagination, but strange things immediately started happening to him as well. Finally they returned it to its original spot in the attic. Some things are better left undisturbed.

It's not all bad having a haunted establishment. The employees swear that a generous phantom has been secretly leaving hefty tips at the bar. Once in a while, a lone $10 bill has been found in the tip jar by the lucky person who opens. Maybe it's from the ghost of the former barmaid, who knows how greatly appreciated those sizable tips are. Or maybe it's from an eternally grateful regular—a "frequent flier" of sorts. Or it could be from Captain John Stone himself. If you turn around very slowly, you'll see him staring intently at you, as if waiting to see your reaction to the tip. That would explain the mischievous glint in his eye that many mistake for a glare.

The Old Powder House

The Old Powder House at the Nathan Tufts Park in Somerville was built in 1704 by shipwright Jean Maillet, but today it's owned by the city of Somerville and operated under the auspices of the Historic Preservation Commission. The round stone tower, which was originally built as a windmill, has a long and colorful history—and a ghost story to boot.

In 1747, the Maillets sold their stone mill to the province of Massachusetts to use for gunpowder storage. That was when it became known as the Powder House—an important munitions depot during the American Revolution. But in 1818, the state began storing gunpowder at other locations and sold the property to a farmer named Peter Tufts, whose sons and descendants became prominent citizens of the city during the 1800s. In fact, the park was named for Peter's son Nathan, founder of Nathan Tufts and Sons, and Nathan's uncle Charles Tufts is the namesake of the nearby Tufts University. In the 1870s, George Emerson purchased the Powder House in which to store his locally popular Emerson's Old Powder House Brand Pickles. By 1972, the Powder House had earned a reputation as the oldest stone building in Massachusetts and was featured on Somerville's new city seal, in honor of the city's one hundredth birthday. A few years later, the park was listed on the National Register of Historic Places, and in 1985, it was designated as a local historic district. The Old Powder House was damaged by fire in 1998, but the city quickly restored it. After all, it's the park's most significant historic feature and conversation piece. You see, somewhere along the line, a legend was born . . .

According to legend, something so unfortunate happened in the mill's loft many years ago that it left a permanent imprint in the atmosphere. One version of the story tells of a young woman, disguised as a man, who sought refuge in the loft one night. But somehow a man who was up to no good discovered that she was actually a woman and tried to molest her. In the process, he became entangled in the mill's machinery and died. His restless spirit is said to still haunt the Powder House today.

The other version is perhaps more accurate, if only because it was told closer to the date of the alleged incident. According to Charles Skinner in *Myths and Legends of Our Own Land*, it was a young woman's beloved father who died after an injury in the tower, and he is the one who haunted it—and may still haunt it today. That account follows:

> The "old powder-house," as the round stone tower is called, that stands on a gravel ridge in Somerville is so named because, at the outbreak of the Revolutionary War, it was used temporarily as a magazine; but long before that, it was a wind-mill. Here in the old days two lovers held their tryst: a sturdy and honest young farmer of the neighborhood and the daughter of a man whose wealth puffed him with purse-pride. It was the plebeian state of the farmer that made him look at him with an unfavorable countenance, and when it was whispered to him that the young people were meeting each other almost every evening at the mill, he resolved to surprise them there and humiliate, if he did not punish, them. From the shadow of the door, they saw his approach, and, yielding to the girl's imploring, the lover secreted himself while she climbed to the loft. The flutter of her dress caught the old man's eye and he hastened, panting, into the mill. For some moments, he groped about, for his eyes had not grown used to the darkness of the place, and hearing his muttered oaths, the girl crept backward from the stair.
>
> She was beginning to hope that she had not been seen, when her foot caught in a loose board and she stumbled, but in her fall, she threw out her hand to save herself and found a rope within her

grasp. Directly that her weight had been applied to it, there was a whir and a clank. The cord had set the great fans in motion. At the same moment, a fall was heard, then a cry, passing from anger into anguish. She rushed down the stair, the lover appeared from his hiding place at the same moment, and together they dragged the old man to his feet. At the moment when the wind had started the sails, he had been standing on one of the millstones, and the sudden jerk had thrown him down. His arm caught between the grinding surfaces and had been crushed to a pulp. He was carried home and tenderly nursed, but he did not live long; yet before he died, he was made to see the folly of his course, and he consented to the marriage that it had cost him so dear to try to prevent. Before she could summon heart to fix the wedding-day, the girl passed many months of grief and repentance, and for the rest of her life, she avoided the old mill. There was good reason for doing so, people said, for on windy nights, the spirit of the old man used to haunt the place, using such profanity that it became visible in the form of blue lights, dancing and exploding about the building.

Blessed Mother Apparition

The Virgin Mary has made divine appearances, known as Marian Apparitions, around the world since the time of her death. Often, such apparitions are preceded by or occur simultaneously with enigmatic images of a religious nature. These have included apparitions of angels, heavenly cloud formations and strange weather phenomena like that experienced by Jesus on the cross, the mysterious appearance of doorways (presumably to Heaven), and inexplicable cross formations. For example, when the Blessed Mother made her remarkable appearance in a window on the third floor of Milton Hospital in 2003, scores of witnesses observed a distinct cross on the hospital's chimney at the same time. But nothing could compete with the crystal-clear image in the window's glass of the Madonna cradling the Christ Child.

Word of the sighting spread so quickly when it first appeared in June 2003 that the hospital administration was forced to seek assistance from the Archdiocese of Boston on how to proceed with such a holy vision and deal with the crowds, which measured easily into the thousands. Out of respect for the patients and nearby residents, those wishing to view the holy image in the window were asked to visit only between 5:30 and 8:30 P.M. Hospital officials purportedly told the *Boston Globe* that the image was nothing but a chemical deposit inside the window, and others said it was condensation between the two panes of glass. Perhaps the chemical deposit or condensation was divinely placed. Unfortunately, the window panes were in an inaccessible location that hindered further investigation. But even skeptics agreed that whatever it was bore a remarkable—if not downright uncanny—resemblance to the Virgin Mary and Child. It was certainly beautiful, by all accounts.

If you're still not so sure someone Upstairs was (or is) watching over Milton and the surrounding greater Boston area, another Blessed Virgin Mary incident occurred on the opposite side of Boston in the town of Medford in March 2004. In that case, a statue of the Blessed Mother outside of the Sacred Heart Church was seen crying. The church was set to close soon, and one theory was that Mary's tears were related to the closing of that church (and others) and to the current scandal rocking the Catholic Church.

Southern
Massachusetts

SOUTHERN MASSACHUSETTS INCLUDES THE SOUTH SHORE (PLYMOUTH County) and the Southeastern region (Bristol County.) The South Shore follows Boston Harbor all the way down through Plymouth County to the edge of the Cape Cod region. Though the South Shore area is endowed more historically than it is paranormally, its neighboring regions, Cape Cod and Southeastern Massachusetts, are two of the most haunted in the state. The latter is home to the outrageously supernatural vicinity known as the Bridgewater Triangle, where mischievous apparitions thumb for rides and terrorize passing motorists, ghost teachers conduct classes for ghost students, old Indian spirits shout out commands, spectral voices bounce instantaneously from one location to the next, and inexplicable sightings of peculiar animals, UFOs, spirit lights, and phantom fires abound. Every story included in this section, therefore, took place within the Bridgewater Triangle save one—the tale of the infamous Lizzie Borden House in Fall River, just north of the triangle, without which no legitimate book about haunted Massachusetts would be complete.

The Bridgewater Triangle

In the 1980s, Loren Coleman, author of *Mysterious America,* coined the name the "Bridgewater Triangle" to designate a triangular region in southern Massachusetts brimming with paranormal phenomena, much like the famous Bermuda Triangle, but with even more diversity. The Massachusetts triangle is roughly two hundred square miles in size, with its corners being Abington, Freetown, and the very haunted Rehoboth. Other well-publicized areas of supernatural activity within the triangle itself include—but are certainly not limited to—the towns of Bridgewater, Taunton, Dighton, Berkley, and the formidable Hockomock Swamp at the heart of the Bridgewater Triangle. As you approach the Bridgewater Triangle, there should be signs warning you that you are really about to enter the Twilight Zone . . .

Massachusetts has several hot spots where ghosts run rampant; however, the Bridgewater Triangle plays host not only to phantoms, but also to UFOs, Yeti-type creatures, demon dogs, monster-size snakes and birds, cryptozoological enigmas, dirt circles (as opposed to crop circles), and other inexplicable atmospheric oddities. For that reason, many believe that the triangle is an immense window to another dimension. Low-flying, unidentified spacecraft have been reported since at least 1760 in the towns of Roxbury, Bridgewater, East Bridgewater, Taunton, and Middleboro. Perhaps the spaceships' pilots etched their identities into Dighton Rock in Berkley, for lack of a better explanation for the strange glyphics blanketing that well-known boulder. Atmospheric anomalies have included "spook lights," also known as ghost lights or orbs, which are simply balls of spirit energy. Various colors of orbs have been seen bouncing along Elm Street in Bridgewater, zigzagging along Raynham's railroad and dog tracks, and drifting about in several areas of Rehoboth. There was also the well-documented day during Colonial times that the clear, blue skies over the entire region turned sulfuric yellow, a meteorological oddity of that time—or of *any* time.

A lot of strange creatures have been seen in Hockomock Swamp, the fifty-two-hundred-acre heart of the Bridgewater Triangle. From man-birds to giant snakes to demon dogs to skeleton ghosts, there's just something about the surroundings that seems to attract—or breed—peculiar critters. But the dense, primeval swamp is booby-trapped with quicksand and muskrat traps, though neither is suitable for capturing the most wanted critter of all—Massachusetts' own version of Bigfoot, the Hockomock Swamp Creature. In the 1970s and 1980s, there was a wave of Bigfoot sightings in Bridgewater, which is on the edge of the swamp. Alarmed residents described the creature as bearlike or apelike, lumbering, towering, hairy, and—for those who managed to get close enough—stinky (must have been the stagnant quicksand baths). Incredibly, the elusive creature has evaded capture to date, either by hand or on film, and also incredibly, it has left behind nothing to indicate that it ever actually was where it was spotted. But the large number of witnesses beg to differ.

Several years ago, a team of archaeologists found an ancient Native American burial ground dating to 6000 B.C. on Grassy Island in Hockomock Swamp. When they attempted to excavate the graves, a mysterious substance bubbled up off the skeletons and evaporated, violently reacting to contact with the air after so many millennia—and every photograph taken of the researchers' activities that day came out blank.

"Hockomock" was the name given to the swamp by the indigenous Native Americans, who referred to it as Devil's Swamp and the Place of Spirits. It was a place to be respected and avoided. Clearly, it was sacred ground to the natives, and as such, any disturbance to it is expressly forbidden . . . or all hell could break loose. Maybe that explains the evil canine with glowing red eyes that a resident of Abington saw slaughter two of his ponies. He said the dog was as large as the ponies and seemed not to be of this earth. It could also explain the snakes from the swamp that are said to be as wide as a tree trunk. And it might explain the Thunderbird—a giant, manlike bird with a wingspan of ten to twelve feet said to have attacked humans in ancient times. These prehistoric-type birds have been seen in an area of the swamp coincidentally called "Bird Hill" and in the village of Taunton, one of the towns associated with the swamp.

So many supernatural incidents have been reported in the entire triangle area that some now believe the government's secret "black helicopters" are looking for explanations. The mysterious black helicopters have been making increasing visits, according to area residents. I don't mean to sound like a conspiracy theorist, but any time mutilated cattle seem to have dropped out of the sky and nobody knows where they came from or to whom they belong, and UFO traffic is simultaneously heavy, you can be sure the legendary men in black will be sent to figure out what's going on before Joe Public does.

The Rock of Ages

Berkley's enigmatic Dighton Rock was located on Assonet Neck on the Taunton River, where it greeted the earliest visitors to America's shores and served as a guestbook of sorts. Because of the irreversible effect of weathering on the oldest markings, the boulder was moved to the protective shelter of Dighton Rock Museum north of Fall River in 1973, thus preserving its remaining inscriptions. But who exactly signed it is a mystery that has never been solved, like many other puzzles born in the numinous region known as the Bridgewater Triangle.

According to Elias Nason and George Varney's *Massachusetts Gazetteer* (1890), the curious inscriptions "have greatly puzzled the antiquaries of both the old and the new world. The rock is eleven feet in length by four and one-half feet in height and consists of a mass of gray granite lying on the sides of the river, which partially covers it at every tide. On the water side, the face of the rock is nearly smooth and is inclined sixty degrees. The figures are rudely carved and partially obliterated near the base by the action of the water." The markings "consist of rude outlines of human heads and bodies, crosses, misshapen letters, broken lines, and other singular forms and combinations."

Since at least 1677, when Puritan leader Cotton Mather copied the inscriptions and sent them to London to be interpreted, many people have tried to decipher the medley of strange glyphs on the face of the stone. So far, nobody has cracked the code, if there is a code. Some scholars claim to have deciphered portions of the stories, based on their own personal expertise with any given language, but nobody has pulled it all together in a comprehensive understanding of what every single marking says and who each inscriber was. The difficulty lies in the fact that the markings on the stone span thousands of years, and the presumed signatures came from people the world over—and maybe even a few from out of this world, by the looks of some of the unusual drawings!

The general consensus is that the carvings are a hodgepodge of ancient Phoenician petroglyphs, Portuguese names, Roman letters, primitive Native American and aboriginal drawings, Colonial signatures, and Norse inscriptions. Suffice it to say, nobody knows how long this remarkable "rock of ages" was used as a message board, but its prominent position on the shore of the Taunton apparently drew people to it like a magnet for several millennia. Every explorer, it seems, dutifully left his mark on Dighton Rock.

Phantom Fires at Anawan Rock

Anawan Rock is located in Squannakonk Swamp on U.S. Route 44 in Rehoboth and is historically famous for the skirmish that took place there. A marker at the foot of the giant boulder states that it is the site where the elderly Anawan—Wampanoag Indian chief and King Philip's war captain—was captured by Captain Benjamin Church of the Colonial army in 1676. His surrender, based on Church's empty promise that he would be treated fairly, marked the end of the yearlong King Philip's War. The old chief's campfire at the foot of Anawan Rock had barely stopped smoldering when the trusting soul was executed in Plymouth, even after being told in the verbal agreement that he and his small band of natives would be spared.

Many people have seen phantom smoke and transient campfires near the site, while others claim to have smelled it. Mysterious smokelike haze found in numerous photographs taken there seems to corroborate that observation. Sorrowful chants are said to bounce off the walls of the forest and bedrock that bears Anawan's name. Some have described it as coming from one direction at one moment and another direction a split second later, lending a supernatural ambience to the atmosphere. It's as if the proud Indian chief changed his mind about going with Church and remains eternally at his campsite.

Other unexplained sounds have been heard as well: screaming, shouting, and even a single word, well emphasized twice—Iootash. Incredibly, *Iootash* is Algonquin for "Stand and fight," and it's a phrase Anawan himself purportedly used at the battle near Mount Hope. Maybe his regretful spirit wishes he'd done that instead of surrendering as he did. Of course, the poor man who heard the phantom's command while alone in the woods had no idea what the unusual word meant at the time, or that Anawan had ever used it. All he knew was that the unseen entity that shouted at him was too close for comfort, so instead of standing and fighting, he skedaddled.

Shad Factory Mill Ruins

Of all the spooky places in the town of Rehoboth—and there are many—none instills a sense of foreboding as potent and memorable as the old Shad Factory Mill ruins. The mill started as the Palmer River Manufacturing Company, built in 1810 on the site of the old Joshua Smith gristmill. The Palmer River mill made cotton yarn until its 1826 expansion, when it began manufacturing fine cotton cloth. At that time, it became the Orleans Manufacturing Company. The Orleans Manufacturing mill was destroyed by fire in 1831 but was rebuilt a year later. Production was halted during the Civil War and resumed when the war was over. Cotton products continued to be manufactured until the second, and final, fire of 1884, which leveled the mill. It was never rebuilt and fell into ruins. But some say the fires that twice destroyed the mill still appear occasionally, even though the mill itself has long since disappeared.

Phantom flames have materialized sporadically and dissipated before incredulous observers. And that's not all . . . Passersby have reported seeing apparitions, including a menacing, hooded male spirit who appears and disappears before their eyes. Mysterious white lights have been seen in the surrounding woods—far easier on the nerves than the occasional screams heard emanating from the ruins. But the most commonly reported phenomenon is not as outwardly blatant. It's a feeling of sadness and anxiety that overwhelms you when simply passing by the ruins, the sensation of being watched by a dark force that doesn't want you there, and the urgent desire to flee quickly.

Haunted Hornbine School

The town of Rehoboth opened the first school in this fledgling nation in 1643, earning it the honor of being dubbed the "Birthplace of Public Education." But it was the Hornbine School, built in 1845, that really put the town's educational facilities on the map. Hornbine is one of Massachusetts' most haunted schools.

The school operated as a one-room schoolhouse for students in kindergarten through ninth grade, but it ceased operation in 1937, when the town eliminated all but three school districts. After serving a number of purposes, Hornbine eventually became vacant, but it was restored to its original appearance by the Hornbine School Association in 1968 and is now open to school groups and to the general public, by appointment. It is in this capacity that the school, located at 144 Hornbine Road, came to be known as haunted. It is said that a stern phantom teacher still holds classes for her equally phantasmal students.

Many people claim to have had paranormal encounters while walking past—or peering into—the unoccupied school. Voices, as if class is being held, are heard emanating from inside, even though passersby can find no source for the noises. Those peeking in the windows have noticed a dramatic drop in temperature surrounding them—a sure sign of ghostly presence. If they stuck around long enough to get a good look inside, they might have seen the strange reddish glow sometimes reported. Most startling of all, though, is the case of a woman who, herself a teacher, was doing a little snooping around on the grounds, just to see what an old-time school looked like. She thought she had chanced onto a history presentation when she peeked through the window to see a teacher and a whole classroom of attentive students dressed in nineteenth-century clothing. The teacher looked out at her rather sternly, as if to admonish the woman for interrupting their session. But the woman wasn't deterred. She walked around the building to the door and found it locked, which was a bit odd (but not as odd as the fact that all those people were inside, yet hers was the only vehicle on the property). She knocked, but nobody answered. Then she walked back to the window through which she had first seen the class and found the schoolhouse completely empty. As she walked away, dazed and confused, she gave the school one last look and saw that the teacher had reappeared and was looking out at her. Seconds later, the teacher evaporated into thin air.

The Red-Headed Hitchhiker

As one of the towns that mark the Bridgewater Triangle's three corners, Rehoboth has more than its fair share of ghost stories. In fact, many people believe it to be the most haunted little town in Massachusetts. It *is* possible. In a town where phantoms leap out of ruins, ghost fires rage, and spectral classes continue long after a deserted old schoolhouse has closed its doors, anything's possible. Take the red-headed hitchhiker, for instance . . .

Once upon a time, a red-headed man wearing a red flannel shirt wandered gingerly along U.S. Route 44 in Rehoboth. Something must have gone awry, because the man who moseyed along the road has now been haunting it for years, terrifying drivers even to this day who dare to brave the deserted stretch of road near the Seekonk-Rehoboth line. Nobody knows who the red-headed man is, or why he gets such a kick out of taunting his unsuspecting victims. Is it because he stepped into the path of an oncoming vehicle long ago and was killed, or because he was involved in a fatal car accident or farming accident nearby? But why seek revenge on (or closure from) hapless strangers? The man clearly knows he's dead, and he uses it to his full advantage. Such shamelessness has made his appearances legendary.

There have been many reports about the red-headed hitchhiker, and all are remarkably similar, giving pause to the notion that the story is pure myth. Every person who has ever been graced with the apparition's presence agrees that his hair is unmistakably red, as is his flannel shirt. Sometimes the middle-aged ghost looks well-groomed, other times he appears disheveled—but his hair and shirt are always, always red. His eye color varies, however, according to his many acquaintances. They've been described as black, lifeless (obviously), glowing, empty, red, yellow, green, white, mischievous, evil, insane, and unnatural. But never have they been described as normal, at least not in hindsight. Usually, he appears so solid that he's managed to get a lift by helpful citizens, only to disappear before their eyes. It seems the phantom enjoys seeing his victims squirm when they ask him a question and he refuses to say anything, offer-

ing instead just a grin and a wicked twinkle in his chameleon eyes. One man told him to get out after such an encounter, at which point the phantom obligingly vanished in an instant.

The phantom of Route 44 has done many things that would be impossible, not to mention plain stupid, if he were not a ghost. He has walked into the path of oncoming vehicles, which proceeded to drive right through him, much to the drivers' horror. In one case, after the driver realized he must have run over a ghost, the redheaded hitchhiker transported himself instantly to a point farther ahead, where he could again walk in front of the same car. He plastered his mug to the passenger-side window of another car being driven at fifty-five miles per hour, but vanished as soon as the driver pulled over.

In yet another case, he sat by the side of the road waiting for his victim to approach by foot, and then he just stared at the man, without responding to questions. As the hapless man hurried away—realizing that something wasn't right about the stranger by the side of the road—he heard menacing laughter bellowing from behind him, then to the left, then to the right, and way up in front of him, and back behind him again, as if it were jumping from place to place instantaneously. Surrounded by the supernatural laughter, he raced back to his broken-down vehicle and found his girlfriend hysterical—she said a strange man's voice had come over their radio saying her name, then laughing repeatedly.

The fiery ghost with the fiery hair always makes himself heard as he disappears. It could be his intimidating laughter, a holler, or even a patronizing statement intended to belittle his victims. But so far, he hasn't said, "Didn't your mother ever tell you not to pick up strangers?"

Rehoboth Village Cemetery

It's a balmy summer night. You're driving down U.S. Route 44 in the town of Rehoboth, a little on edge thinking about that redheaded hitchhiker guy known to prowl this stretch of highway. Your senses are already on full alert as you pass by the Village Cemetery, when suddenly a bloodcurdling scream pierces the darkness, followed by an ungodly, maniacal fit of laughter. Whatever you do, don't stop to investigate—especially if your name is Catherine.

Rehoboth Village Cemetery dates to the 1600s, but its most famous resident—resident ghost, that is—dresses in eighteenth-century clothing. He's an older man who appears in the rear southwest corner of the cemetery, alternately laughing hysterically and crying inconsolably at one particular grave. He sneers at anyone who dares to look his way and seems to take pleasure in scaring away visitors. The feisty phantom with empty, dark eye sockets spews forth vulgarities at members of the gentler sex and follows such verbal lashings with obscene gestures that apparently have endured several centuries. He especially targets women. In fact, he may have bludgeoned a woman to death when he was alive. One witness to his apparition heard him scream, "Catherine, Catherine!" in her direction, followed by unprintable expletives. She fled the cemetery in terror, actually fearing for her life. Glancing back in her rearview window at the spot where she had seen him, she noticed that he was leaning over a woman in Victorian garb who was lying on the ground, and he was pounding furiously on her . . . then they both vanished before her eyes.

Other witnesses have reported an old man in the cemetery screaming and pounding on their car windows as they sped away, and several reports have an old man gliding through the cemetery looking for victims to terrorize. His movement has been described as liquidlike and deliberate. Cold spots are commonly reported throughout the cemetery, and other voices have been heard, such as a young girl's ghostly laughter on the opposite side of the cemetery.

The Rehoboth Village Cemetery is not the only haunted graveyard in the small town. Palmer River Burial Ground on Lake Street is also known to be quite haunted. A young boy dressed in nineteenth-century clothing has been seen wandering through the cemetery, as if looking for help. Sometimes a boy fitting that description is seen accompanied by two grown men, and a phantom coffin has also been reported, appearing and disappearing from the center of the burial grounds. It seems that in Rehoboth's cemeteries, it's hard for a body to "rest in peace."

Lizzie Borden House

Thirty-two-year-old Lizzie Borden was accused of murdering her well-to-do father and stepmother on August 4, 1892, in their modest house at 92 Second Street in Fall River. After the grisly murders, which were committed with either an ax or a hatchet, the 1845 house became a city landmark and continued to be used as a private residence for the next hundred years or so. Though Lizzie was acquitted of the murders due to a lack of evidence, she continued to be ostracized by her community—and indeed, the whole world. So she changed her name to Lizbeth and moved a mile away to a fourteen-room mansion called Maplecroft in the elite Heritage Hill neighborhood, compliments of her substantial inheritance. She died alone in 1927, within ten days of her sister and staunchest supporter, Emma. The two women were buried in the family plot. That had to make their parents roll over in their graves!

The Borden residence on Second Street eventually became a bed-and-breakfast and is currently owned by Donald Woods and managed by his partner, Lee Ann Wilbur. Today the brave and curious can tour the infamous house and even sleep in Lizzie Borden's bedroom—or in Abby and Andrew's bedroom, where Abby was nearly decapitated by nineteen sharp blows to the head, before her husband suffered the same fate with eleven blows that virtually sheared off his face. The house has been restored to its humble Victorian appearance at the time of the double homicide; many of the Borden family's belongings are still there. The breakfast served to lodgers is the same that the Bordens themselves ate the morning of their murders. If that isn't authentic enough for Lizzie buffs, perhaps the ghosts of Abby and Andrew will make it so.

Many guests have reported hearing a woman weeping during the night, and some have said they were tucked in by a kindly older woman wearing old-fashioned clothing—even though such pampering "wasn't part of their package." Objects occasionally move by themselves as stunned onlookers watch. Lights sometimes flicker, as they should in any reputable haunted home, and cameras and video equipment malfunction, much to the delight of those who know that such things are a sure sign of paranormal activity.

Visit www.Lizzie-Borden.com for more information. For those brave enough to stay at the Lizzie Borden Bed and Breakfast, be forewarned that if the tragic history of the house doesn't give you a severe case of the willies, the ghost stories surely will.

Cape Cod and the Islands

CAPE COD LOOKS LIKE A GIANT ARM EXTENDING OUT FROM AMERICA into the Atlantic Ocean, with Sandwich and Barnstable at its shoulder and Provincetown at its fist. It seems as if nearly every one of the 250-plus bed-and-breakfasts on the Cape is said to be haunted—enough ghosts to easily satisfy the heavy volume of seasonal traffic. With eleven million tourists now visiting the region each year, it's no wonder there's been such a recent deluge of ghost stories, as more and more people are being exposed to Cape Cod's ghosts.

The neighboring islands of Martha's Vineyard and Nantucket are not without their own share of ghost stories; the residents just don't like to admit it, as opposed to Cape Cod inhabitants, who boast of their ghosts. But ghosts and UFOs have definitely gotten up close and personal with the rich and famous on the state's two largest islands.

The Barnstable House

The famously haunted Barnstable House at 3010 Main Street in Barnstable is no longer an actual residence, but an office building that houses a number of Cape Cod–area businesses and agencies. You would never know by looking at it from the road that the impeccable structure is nearly three hundred years old. And you *certainly* would never know by looking at it how incredibly haunted it is—or at least, was.

Many of the haunted happenings at the Barnstable House have involved fire, in one way or another. In 1975, the local volunteer fire department was called to the house, which was an inn at the time, to find the source of heavy smoke that was pouring from the roof. The firefighters performed a thorough search but found no fire; however, they did find dense smoke in the attic, so they cleared the mysterious smoke and prepared to leave. As they were standing outside, several of them spotted a peculiar woman in a long white gown, the same woman they thought they had seen in an upstairs window but were unable to find inside. Some said she had long brown hair, but others said it was blond. The woman drifted fluidly among the men, asking strange questions. In hindsight, they agreed that she seemed to be drifting *too* fluidly—as if she were hovering several inches above the snow. The firemen really didn't give the woman much thought at the time, though, because the night air was dark and thick with smoke and fog, and there was so much activity. Their eyes might have just been playing tricks on them. But back at the station, they compared notes and had to admit that nothing about the woman made sense, and nothing about the mysterious smoke that had no source made sense either.

Another fire-related incident involved a rowdy group of high school students who were given permission to spend the night and take infrared photographs in the dark to see if they could capture the alleged ghosts of the house on film. The owner was in bed listening to the ruckus when a fire started up in her fireplace out of the blue, and was it roaring! Sensing that one of the spirits was angry about the noisy students, she called out for the kids to settle down. As soon as they did, the fire shrank, and when the students finally fell silent, the fire went out completely at exactly the same moment.

Then there was the time that a mother and son, who could see dead people, were guests at the inn. The little boy drew a picture of the inn with fire—and ghosts—shooting out its windows. He showed it to the caretaker at the time and told her the ghosts were terrible and wanted to burn the house down. After the boy and his mother left to settle in for the night, the caretaker went downstairs and found an old candle brightly lit. She hadn't lit it, but she blew it out. A few minutes later, when she was walking by the same candle, she found it again burning brightly. This happened four consecutive times.

Other things went on in the house, too. Doors mysteriously slammed shut, and people could feel cold spots when climbing up the staircase. A rocking chair rocked by itself in front of the fireplace. But one of the strangest incidents occurred one day when a man dressed in Colonial clothing walked through the bar area with an old-time tray and empty glasses, as if he worked there. One impressed guest applauded the owner of the inn for such authenticity in his employees, but then was quite taken aback to learn that the inn had no such employees.

Several people have died on the premises, including a young girl who drowned in a stream that ran under the house and a previous owner who hanged himself from a tree on the property. Also, several owners and their family members died peacefully in the home over the years as they passed it down from generation to generation. Any number of spirits may have haunted the house at any given time. But if any are still there, they are virtually imperceptible, subtly coexisting with the many businesses whose offices are now in the remarkable house.

The Old Yarmouth Inn

When Arpad Voros and his wife, Sheila FitzGerald, purchased the Old Yarmouth Inn at 223 Route 6A in Yarmouth Port in 1996, they were naive about the spirit world. The previous owner had told them the inn was haunted, but the couple didn't really buy into such silliness. Their place was much too cozy to harbor a ghost. Ghosts belonged in scary, foreboding, dingy old houses on treeless hilltops, not in such a fine establishment as the Old Yarmouth. Boy, were they wrong, and they're not afraid to admit it now.

The first proof that it was haunted under the new owners' tenure was when Sheila's sister, Maureen, went down to the kitchen early one morning, before anyone else had been up, and was stunned to find that the bread mixer had somehow turned itself on. Another morning, a customer was heading to the kitchen to help herself to coffee. She stopped at the swinging doors to figure out which was the in door and which was the out, when she heard a muffled voice tell her to "push." Then one night, when

Sheila, Maureen, and Arpad were having dinner in the tavern, the window next to their table began moaning and rattling without provocation and then fell silent.

That's not the only thing that has rattled on the premises. One man who was spending the night in one of the four guest rooms was awakened one night when he felt someone sit on his bed, but nobody was there—so he pulled the blankets up over his head. Moments later, he felt his feet being massaged by icy hands, even though they were tucked well under the blankets. And if that wasn't bad enough, the attention-seeking phantom grabbed onto the bedposts at the foot of the bed and started shaking the bed, until the poor guest fled from the room and waited out on the deck until morning, when he told Sheila and Arpad about his hair-raising experience. By then, they had experienced enough to know better than to dismiss the man's story as fabrication; it just sounded so . . . dramatic. But then Arpad's ninety-year-old mother came out on the deck to join them and said she couldn't sleep because of all the rattling and clanging going on in that particular guest's room that night.

The Old Yarmouth's menu covers include even more ghost stories that Sheila wrote up. She shared the following with me:

> There was a stack of ashtrays at the end of the bar. We were startled when one of the ashtrays slipped off the top of a stack, but thought nothing of it, until the ashtray zoomed down the length of the bar.
>
> Several years ago, a party of ten came into the tavern for dinner. These people were not regulars, and I wanted to go over to the table and welcome them. I had just finished a conversation with an adjoining table about the Inn and recent ghost sightings when the older woman at the end of the new group's table announced that ghosts do not exist and anyone who thought they did should have their heads examined. We all laughed, and then, without explanation, the front cover of the air conditioner fell off, and instead of dropping to the floor, it sailed through the air and grazed the top of the woman's head some eight feet away!
>
> In October 2003, we hosted a series of séances that were merely theatrical performances, but aroused our ghost nonetheless. The medium spent several days preparing the Red Room to resemble a Victorian Era parlor. On the gas stove in the Red Room, we had a glass vase filled with silk roses and blue marbles. One morning we

found the vase split perfectly into two pieces, yet otherwise intact, laying on the brick hearth on either side of the gas stove. The blue marbles were laid out in front of the hearth in a perfect arch, and the silk roses were fanned out between the marbles. Arpad and I were in awe, and this confirmed our status as reluctant believers!

Paranormal experiences at the historic Old Yarmouth run the gamut from the very mundane to the outright brazen, but each and every one of them adds spice to the already tasty cuisine. Sheila said that their ghosts are never evil or ill-intentioned, just playful and mischievous.

Screeching Hannah Screecham

Back in the days of piracy and witch hysteria, Hannah Screecham lived alone in a humble shanty near Barnstable overlooking Cotuit Bay. The old woman had deep, dark eyes—the kind that paranoid types call black and menacing—and her laugh was like the screech of a seagull. The locals, who at the time were suspicious of anyone a little different than themselves, thought it was odd for a woman to wear a black cloak and keep to herself like Hannah did. Such a fuss they made over the poor woman that the so-called pillars of the community decided to pay her a visit and insist that she leave the area. That did not go over well. Hannah was furious, and her guard dogs, sensing their mistress's anger, chased the men away.

A week later, the entire area was stricken with an epidemic of smallpox. Of course, the locals were sure Hannah had caused it. Again they approached her, but this time they took her forcefully to the courthouse to be tried for witchcraft. The townspeople, who were amassing in an angry mob outside of the courthouse, were so eager to blame someone for their misfortunes that they stormed into the building partway through the trial. They dragged the as-yet-uncharged woman out to a tree, where they promptly hanged her.

Very shortly thereafter, a mysterious pirate and two of his crewmembers arrived in town and cut the lifeless body down, then fled to Noisy Point. When they were finally captured, the pirate admitted to being the woman's son and said he had buried the inno-cent woman somewhere on the point with his cache of treasure. Neither the body nor the treasure has ever been found, but many people believe that Hannah Screecham now haunts Noisy Point, guarding not only her son's treasure, but also the treasure of the famous pirate Captain Kidd, which is also believed to be buried there. An apparition in her likeness has been seen wandering along the shoreline. Nobody knows whether the piercing cry they hear at sunset, even to this day, is her gull-like laughter . . . or her death scream.

Jumping Black Flash

Whoever said black isn't a color obviously never heard of the colorful character known as the Black Flash of Provincetown—also known as the Phantom Fiend, the Black Phantom, or Massachusetts' own version of England's Spring-Heeled Jack. Here is a guy— or something—that stood eight to ten feet tall, dressed in black from head to toe, and flapped his big ugly wings or cape as he leaped over tall fences and pounced down from roadside trees at unsuspecting pedestrians. Some even said he spit blue flames. He terrorized the citizens of Provincetown from 1938 to 1945, delighting in the horror he evoked from each taunting encounter.

It started out with schoolchildren complaining of something big and black that they'd seen lurking behind the dunes, rocks, and trees. When they also added that the black thing had pointy ears and silver, glowing eyes, their stories were dismissed as pure imagination. But when an adult female was accosted by the creature right near the Town Hall, the townspeople took notice. The woman said the creature jumped at her as if on springs, with its cape spread wide like wings in flight. Its black eyes were inhuman, like pits of black fire, and it made an unforgettable, horrible sound like a giant buzzing insect. Hers was the first in a series of encounters by many local residents, young and old, male and female. Typically, the black fiend pounced down from rooftops or treetops directly in front of passersby and stared tauntingly at them. As he fled, leaving his victims paralyzed with fear, his menacing laughter trailed behind him.

The police department drew up a list of tall, athletic types around town who were also known to be jokesters, assuming that they had a nimble jokester on their hands. Needless to say, the list was very short, and eventually every suspect on that list was cleared. Nobody could fathom *what* they had in their midst, but

whatever it was, it was seemingly unstoppable. One man confronted the creature in his backyard when his dog cornered it against his eight-foot fence. He said the phantom just laughed and bounded spryly over the fence like a superhero. Another man tried to bring the phantom down when he encountered it on the town common. But as he threw the first punch, the phantom grabbed his fist and squeezed so hard—all the while laughing his horrible, eerie laughter—that the man collapsed on the ground in agony. With that, the hooded, caped phantom with silver, glowing eyes was off again, eluding all attempts to capture him.

When reports of the creature being cornered in the schoolyard started pouring in at the police department in November 1945, the officers thought it was their lucky day. They would finally unmask the troublesome caped fiend and bring him to justice. They approached the schoolyard quietly and found him cornered up against the fence. The creature took a defiant stance, with hands on hips, and glared at them. As the four officers moved in, warning him not to move, he burst out laughing and effortlessly leaped—like the bionic man—over the school's ten-foot fence. It was hopeless. If Provincetown's finest couldn't bring down their local fiend, then who could? The answer came a few weeks later.

In December 1945, four children were home alone when they spotted the black phantom stealthily approaching their homestead. They hurried inside and grabbed whatever they could find to defend themselves. In a split second, it was at their door, toying with the handle as if to prolong the apprehension it knew its young victims were feeling. But it underestimated the ingenuity of youth. One of the young boys grabbed a pail of hot water and hurried up on the rooftop with it. (Good thing he'd read "The Three Little Pigs.") He tiptoed to the front side of the house until he was standing directly over the black phantom, and then he dropped the bucket of hot water down on the creature and hurried back inside. The children heard the predator gasp, and then it was gone—but this time he spared them his signature laugh. There was nothing to laugh about. He'd been defeated by the most innocent and helpless of all his victims—children. How humiliating for him. Like the big bad wolf, the phantom ran off in shame and has never been seen in Provincetown since.

The Orleans Inn

The Orleans Inn was built in 1875 by Aaron Snow for his family of nine. After Snow and his wife passed away, the building at 3 Old County Road on Nauset Harbor in Orleans sat vacant for nearly a decade. Then in 1900, two business-minded sisters bought it and turned it into a rooming house, where during the Roaring Twenties, it was said, several female boarders came up with their own business idea, entertaining clients in their rooms. Some years later, two prostitutes were murdered on the property—one was shot to death right in the front parking lot. The boardinghouse was sold and resold, passing through many hands, allegedly including the Irish Mafia. Finally, in the 1940s, it was turned into a fine restaurant and inn and prospered. But something was amiss inside, or at least in the lives of the employees working inside. A bartender hanged himself in the cupola, and a dishwasher hanged himself some time later in the basement. Both of those areas reportedly are quite haunted today.

Ed and Laurie Maas purchased the dilapidated inn in 1996 and were planning to level it until they learned of its history—and ghosts—from neighbors. They decided instead to put their hearts and souls, and a couple million bucks, into restoring it to its original Victorian splendor, with the help of their son Ryan and other family members. During renovations, the Maases quickly discovered that the ghost stories were true. Ed occasionally returned to the inn late at night to find the two front doors wide open, even though they were triple-bolted each night at closing. Shadows were seen by construction workers, and doors were known to open and close on their own. Several people have heard a cat mewing, even though the inn had no cats. But word has it that the two old-maid sisters were quite fond of felines and had a number of them living there at any given time. Inexplicable drafts have been felt in conjunction with an intangible sensation of being watched. Heavy footsteps have been heard going down into the basement, and the sound of faint, ethereal voices from the past have been reported. Ed told me that occasionally guests who are not familiar with the history of the inn have come down for breakfast in the morning and asked to hear about the poltergeist, because they sensed a presence and wanted to know more. He said that recently glasses have been observed sliding off tables, "as if being pushed by an invisible source."

One night, after a waitress had blown out all of the candles on the tables, she returned a short time later to the dining area and found every one of them relit and burning brightly. And a previous owner admitted that one night when she was locking up, she said her usual, casual "Goodnight, Fred," to the ghost rumored to haunt the place and was stunned to hear him reply with a teasingly drawn out, "Goodniiiight . . ." There was nobody else in the restaurant that night, but the voice coming from the shadows was as clear as day. One can almost picture the devilish ghost grinning as it considered adding, "Sweet dreeeeeams . . ."

The Hyena Hunt

It appears that in the mid-1800s, a creature not even remotely native to this part of the world terrorized the Cape Cod town of Wellfleet. According to newspaper accounts of the time, "hideous noises" were sometimes heard at night, and strange footprints were found in the sand. Barnyards and chicken coops were under siege, and women and children were afraid to go outside. A massive hunt was organized for an animal believed to be a hyena, based on descriptions provided by those who had glimpsed the awful beast—though none could imagine where such a creature could have come from. Maybe it escaped from the Bridgewater Triangle or, farther west, from the Quabbin Reservoir, both known for their bizarre animal sightings. Or maybe, if it really was a hyena, it had somehow arrived by boat from Africa, India, or the Middle East. Whatever it was, it was never found so that it could be definitively identified. As the hyena hunt went on, the "hideous noises" drifted farther and farther away, until the nights finally became silent once again. But the legend was memorialized in a poem by Dr. Thomas Newcomb Stone in his 1869 book, *Cape Cod Rhymes*. Stone was a Wellfleet physician who enjoyed writing what he called "rhymes," rather than poetry. A portion of his rhyme called "The Hyena Hunt" follows:

> In Wellfleet, when the sun was low,
> All bloodless lay the untrodden snow,
> And dark and dreary was the flow
> Of the Atlantic, dashing ceaselessly.

But Wellfleet saw another sight,
When the horns were blown at morning light,
Assembling men with muskets bright,
To join the hunt, right willingly.

Oh! Few could tell when many met,
When the hunt was o'er, and the sun was set,
With legs well tired, and faces wet,
What *foe* they chased, so valiantly.

And still, as through those woods of pine,
The traveler wends, at eve's decline,
He stands to hear the fearful whine
Of hyena's dreadful mystery.

Some vow it is lioness, bore
By ships from Africa's sunny shore,
That paces now our Cape sands o'er;
Moaning for whelps, most piteously.

Some still, a hyena, whose fearful howl,
Had shook the woods of Tonegal,
In company with the fierce jackal,
Fighting the Fellah, hideously.

Some unbelievers, with taunting sneer,
Swore 'twas a goat, a dog, a deer,
Whose footsteps, magnified by fear,
Had seized the fearful hearted.

But there those fearful footsteps stand,
Imbedded on Atlantic's strand,
And the moaning cry runs through the land,
As if from loved ones parted. . . .

No Little Green Men

The following case was mentioned in Ray Fowler's *Casebook of a UFO Investigator* and is also one of many cases recorded in the Massachusetts MUFON files. On March 27, 1979, a young man was driving down the Edgartown–Oak Bluffs Road on Martha's Vineyard at about 10:00 P.M., when he noticed a green glow coming from behind the sand dunes to his right. He thought that perhaps it was people using glow sticks on the beach, but the glow brightened, and he was soon able to see the source of the light. In the water offshore was a "luminous green cylinder with rounded ends." The man stopped his car but kept the engine running and realized his radio was picking up a strange, low-frequency humming sound. He watched the object rise slowly out of the water until it was nearly overhead, casting a glow across a wide area of beach and water. He grabbed for a flashlight but was unable to use it, because all he could move was his head. The rest of his body had become temporarily paralyzed. All he could do was watch the object for several minutes, until it sped out of sight. Interestingly, his Timex watch, which he'd been meaning to adjust, was suddenly set correctly and worked accurately for a month following the incident, even though it had been running so fast that it was three days ahead at the time of the UFO sighting.

The young man's story was all the more believable because he was an auxiliary policeman and was well known by the local police force. It was not in his character to exaggerate or make up stories. Even if he'd said little green men came out of the green flying object, nobody at the station would have doubted him. He spoke earnestly and was noticeably shaken when he gave his statement to the Oak Bluffs police. He was an ideal witness, reacting exactly the way one might expect from someone who had just seen a UFO.

UFO Sightings of the Rich and Famous

UFOs are often spotted around Cape Cod and Martha's Vineyard. Even famous folks have admitted to seeing them. Actor Dan Aykroyd mentioned his own 1986 UFO sighting in a review he wrote for David Sereda's *Evidence: The Case for NASA UFOs.* He and his wife were at their home in Chilmark on the island of Martha's Vineyard, when they witnessed two flying objects he described as "tiny, perfectly round, luminous bodies" traveling "in tandem at high velocity." Two guests staying with them at the time also saw the UFOs. There was no logical explanation for what they all saw—they agreed the objects weren't airplanes, helicopters, planets, shooting stars, satellites, or any other airborne object known to them. The sighting confirmed Aykroyd's lifelong belief that UFOs do exist.

Other prominent names have *not* admitted to seeing them. Yet rumor has it that a certain U.S. president whose family compound is in Hyannisport bore witness to a genuine alien spacecraft from aboard his pleasure cruiser one day. According to a family member who was there, everyone on board saw a large, disk-shaped, metallic gray object come toward the president's boat. It made no sound and had no noticeable means of propulsion. The object hovered for less than a minute—while Secret Service agents scrambled about helplessly—before zooming out of sight. That event effectively cut the pleasure cruise short, and everyone involved was told not to discuss the incident. Our lips are sealed . . .

Setstills

"Don't dawdle along the way, or the setstills will get you!" That's what old-time Nantucketers told their children and grandchildren to make them go straight home for dinner, and the story continues to be passed down through the generations. "Setstills" are ghosts that sit on the fences of Nantucket's cemeteries waiting for innocent victims to walk by so they can grab them. When I was a kid, I heeded warnings of the "earcutter" lurking in the hallway of my grandmother's high-rise apartment building, waiting for mischievous children to try to escape the stuffy senior housing confines, but setstills are a new one for me. You've gotta love the ingenuity of our elders to keep the young whippersnappers in line!

If you're inclined to check out the theory of setstills yourself, the best place to find them is at the Old North Cemetery on New Lane, which is said to be quite haunted. This was once a private burial ground for the Gardner family, but the Nantucket Historical Association became the official caretaker of the property in 1924. Little Abigail Gardner, who died in 1709 and was the first person buried there, is believed to still haunt the cemetery. Children of the island once spoke of a small child's ghost named Mary Abby, who told them she was looking for her father in the cemetery. Could

Mary Abby and Abigail Gardner be one and the same? No stones with either name had been found until the early 1980s, when town crews found a small headstone hidden under some brush in an area of the cemetery they were clearing. It was for a three-year-old girl named Mary Abby. So the children had been right. Such a child *had* existed, and she may still be there today, "setting still" on the fence . . . waiting for you.

Bibliography

Books

Citro, Joseph. *Passing Strange*. Boston, MA: Houghton Mifflin Company, 1996.

Coleman, Loren. *Mysterious America*. London: Faber & Faber, 1983.

Fowler, Raymond. *Casebook of a UFO Investigator*. Englewood Cliffs, NJ: Prentice-Hall, 1981.

Hall, Richard H. *The UFO Evidence*. Washington, D.C.: National Investigations Committee on Aerial Phenomena, 1964.

Jasper, Mark. *Haunted Cape Cod and the Islands*. Yarmouth Port, MA: On Cape Publications, 2002.

———. *Haunted Inns of New England*. Yarmouth Port, MA: On Cape Publications, 2000.

Lasalandra, Michael, and Mark Merenda. *Satan's Harvest*. New York: Dell Publishing Company, 1990.

Macken, Lynda Lee. *Haunted Salem and Beyond*. Forked River, NJ: Black Cat Press, 2001.

Myers, Arthur. *Ghostly Register*. New York: McGraw-Hill/Contemporary Books, 1986.

Nadler, Holly Mascott. *Ghosts of Boston Town*. Camden, ME: Down East Books, 2002.

Pitkin, David J. *Ghosts of the Northeast*. New York: Aurora Publications, 2002.

Robinson, Charles Turek. *The New England Ghost Files*. North Attleboro, MA: Covered Bridge Press, 1994.

Rogers, Barbara Radcliffe, and Stillman Rogers. *Massachusetts—Off the Beaten Path*. Guilford, CT: Globe Pequot Press, 2003.

Sereda, David. *Evidence: The Case for NASA UFOs.* Los Angeles, CA: Terra Entertainment, 2002.

Skinner, Charles M. *Myths and Legends of Our Own Land: Tales of Puritan Land.* Vol. 4. Philadelphia: J. B. Lippincott. 1896.

Stone, Thomas. *Cape Cod Rhymes.* Cambridge, MA: Riverside Press, 1896.

Winthrop, John. *The History of New England from 1630–1649.* James Kendall, ed. New York: Charles Scribners and Sons, 1908.

Online Sources

"Anawan Rock." Home page. Retrieved 21 June 2004. http://home.comcast.net/~johnk4678/anawan/Anawan_Rock.htm.

"The Angry Ghost on the Stairs." *Castle of Spirits.* Retrieved 4 May 2004. http://www.castleofspirits.com/stairs.html.

"Asa Snow aka 'Popcorn Snow.'" *Massachusetts Area Ghost Investigators Coalition.* Retrieved 27 April 2004. http://www.magicghosts.com/investigations/asasnow.html.

Aubeck. "UFOs over Boston." *Statement on Alien Abduction.* Retrieved 11 May 2004. http://www.virtuallystrange.net/ufo/updates/.

Aykroyd, Dan. "Dan Aykroyd Comments on NASA UFOs." *UFO NASA.* Retrieved 11 May 2004. http://www.ufonasa.com/2_Aykroyd.html.

"Aza." *Massachusetts Crossroads.* Retrieved 22 June 2004. http://www.masscrossroads.com/aza.

Belanger, Jeff. "Captain John Stone's Haunted Inn." *Legends of the Supernatural.* Retrieved 19 April 2004. http://www.ghostvillage.com/legends/2002/legends8_12142002.shtml.

"Berkley, Massachusetts, 1890." *Cape Cod History.* Retrieved 23 June 2004. http://www.capecodhistory.us/Mass1890/Berkley1890.htm.

"The Betty Andreasson Encounter." *UFO Casebook.* Retrieved 27 April 2004. http://www.ufocasebook.com/Andreasson.html.

"Beverly, Massachusetts, USA, April 22, 1996." *UFOs at Close Sight.* Retrieved 10 May 2004. http://www.chez.com/lesovnis/htm/beverly66.htm.

"Boston Light History." Page 2. Retrieved 13 July 2004. http://www.lighthouse.cc/boston/history2.html.

"Boston Light—Massachusetts." *Haunted Lighthouses.* Retrieved 13 July 2004. www.angelfire.com/va3/keepthelightsshining/Personal/HauntedLighthouses.html.

"A Brief History of Lines West—The New York, New Haven and Hartford Railroad Co." *Catskill Archive.* Retrieved 8 June 2004. http://www.catskillarchive.com/rrextra/abnere2.html.

Chadwick, Courtney. "Ghostly Hotspots in New England." *Parascope.*

Retrieved 26 April 2004. http://www.parascope.com/articles/ 0797/ghostmain.htm.

"Charlesgate." *Massachusetts Crossroads.* Retrieved 22 June 2004. http://www.masscrossroads.com/cgate.

"Christmas Shoppers Watch a UFO Fly over Boston." *UFO Roundup.* Retrieved 5 May 2004. http://www.westmassmufon.org/ uforoundup3.htm.

"Craft of Mystery Finally Tracked to Its Lair—Perhaps!" Project 1947. Retrieved 5 May 2004. http://www.project1947.com/fig/1909a.htm.

"Creature Seen Moving Stones and Small Pieces of Wood." Report #1199 (Class A)—BFRO. Retrieved 27 April 2004. http://www.bfro.net/ GDB/show_report.asp?ID = 1199&PrinterFriendly + True.

"The Curse of the Charles Haskell." *Researchers and Investigators of the Paranormal.* Retrieved 30 April 2004. http://riptx.net/ charleshaskell.htm.

"The Curse of Giles Corey." *Haunted Salem.* Retrieved 27 April 2004. http://www.hauntedsalem.com/hauntinghistory/gilescorey.html.

"Dana—Ghost Town." Home page. Retrieved 8 June 2004. http://www.ghosttowns.com/states/ma/dana.html.

"Did a UFO Buzz Lunenburg?" *The UFO Casebook.* Retrieved 21 June 2004. http://www.ufocasebook.com/82402.html.

"Dighton Rock, Massachusetts." Home page. Retrieved 27 April 2004. http://members.skyweb.net/~channy/dighton.html.

"Dillingham House." *Home and Garden Television: Historic/Landmarks.* Retrieved 19 July 2004. http://www.hgtv.com/hgtv/ah_travel_ landmarks/article/0,1801,HGTV_3217_1392584,00.html.

"Dover Demon." *The Cryptozoo: Weird Predators Petting Zoo!* Retrieved 27 April 2004. http://www.parascope.com/en/cryptozoo/ predators05.htm.

"Dover Demon." *Metareligion.* Retrieved 27 April 2004. http://www.meta-religion.com/Paranormale/Cryptozoology/ Humanoid/dover_demon.htm.

"The Dover Demon." Home page. Retrieved 27 April 2004. http://www.geocities.com/chrisandjenna441/ddemon.html.

"The Dover Demon." *Strange New England.* Retrieved 30 April 2004. http://strangene.com/monsters.dover.htm.

"Dungeon Rock." *Friends of Lynn Woods.* Retrieved 8 July 2004. http://www.flw.org/2950.htm.

"Dungeon Rock." *Massachusetts Area Ghost Investigators Coalition.* Retrieved 8 July 2004. http://www.magicghosts.com/investigations/ DUNGEON.html.

Ely, Dina. "Haunted Nantucket." *Nantucket Island.* Retrieved 15 July 2004. http://www.suite101.com/article.cfm/nantucket_island/103531.

"Emissaries of God." *Mysteries*. Retrieved 15 June 2004.
    http://www.mysteries.pwp.blueyonder.co.uk/3,9.htm.
"Eunice Williams Covered Bridge." *Shadowlands Haunted Places Index—Massachusetts*. Retrieved 8 June 2004.
    http://www.theshadowlands.net/places/massachusetts.htm.
"Faithful See Image of Virgin Mary in Hospital Window." *Researchers and Investigators of the Paranormal*. Retrieved 27 July 2004.
    http://riptx.net/vmary.htm.
"Family Excursions—'Ghoulies and Ghosties.'" *Yesterday's Island*.
    Retrieved 15 July 2004. http://www.yesterdaysisland.com/
    family_xmas/ghosts.html.
Famous Quotes on UFOs. Retrieved 11 May 2004. http://www.prodigy.net/
    thr-ok/quotes.html.
"Federal Government." *Massachusetts Crossroads*. Retrieved 22 June 2004.
    http://www.masscrossroads.com/fedgov.
Fyden, Anthony. "The Eunice Williams Covered Bridge." *The Five Most Haunted Places in the Berkshire Hills*. Retrieved 20 April 2004.
    http://lenox.iberkshires.com/story.php?story_id = 12499.
———. "Houghton Mansion/Masonic Lodge, North Adams—Chauffeur John Widders." *The Five Most Haunted Places in the Berkshire Hills*.
    Retrieved 20 April 2004. http://lenox.iberkshires.com/
    story.php?story_id + 12499.
"The Ghost from the Old Yarmouth Inn." *Old Yarmouth Inn Restaurant and Tavern*. Retrieved 28 April 2004.
    http://www.oldyarmouthinn.com/ghoststories.html.
"The Gloucester Sea Serpent." *Metareligion*. Retrieved 27 April 2004.
    http://www.meta-religion.com/Paranormale/Cryptozoology/
    Sea_Monsters/gloucester_sea_serpent.html.
"The Gloucester Sea Serpent." *Museum of Hoaxes*. Retrieved 27 April
    2004. http://www.museumofhoaxes.com/serpent.html.
Golz, Scott. "Phantom of the Rehoboth Village Cemetery." *PARAseek*.
    Retrieved 23 June 2004. http://www.paraseek.com/invest/
    scottg1.html.
"The Great Train Wrecks." *Trumbull's Early Public Transportation*.
    Retrieved 10 June 2004. http://www.trumbullhistory.org/transprt/.
"Greenfield." *Massachusetts Crossroads*. Retrieved 8 June 2004.
    http://www.masscrossroads.com/janqhits.html.
Hammond Castle Museum. Home page. Retrieved 7 May 2004.
    http://www.hammondcastle.org.
Hanny, Carol. "Bash-Bish Falls." *Bash-Bish Falls, Mt. Washington, Massachusetts*. Retrieved 27 April 2004. http://members.skyweb.net/
    ~ channy/bash.html.
Hansen, Rolf. "The Legend of Chief Graylock." *The Berkshire Web*.

Retrieved 30 April 2004. http://www.berkshireweb.com/sports/
hiking/graylock.html.

———. "The Legend of Chief Greylock." *Mount Greylock—A Berkshire
County Attraction.* Retrieved 8 June 2004. http://www.surfwiz.com/
mount-greylock.htm.

"The Haunted Inn of Concord, Massachusetts." *Concord's Colonial Inn.*
Retrieved 19 April 2004. http://www.concordscolonialinn.com/
haunted-inn.php.

"Hawthorne Cove Marina." Home page. Retrieved 4 May 2004.
http://www.hawthornecove.com/.

Hawthorne Hotel. Home page. Retrieved 4 May 2004.
http://www.hawthornehotel.com/.

"A History of the Park through Time." *Nathan Tufts Park.* Retrieved 26
July 2004. http://www.ci.somerville.ma.us/forms/
NathanParks%20Brochure_10_23.pdf.

"History of Stone's Public House." *Stone's Public House—History.*
Retrieved 19 April 2004. http://www.stonespublichouse.com/
History.asp.

The House of the Seven Gables. Home page. Retrieved 2 June 2004.
http://www.7gables.org/.

"The Investigation of Witch Hollow." *NEPG Ghost File: Witch Hollow.*
Retrieved 4 May 2004. http://www.unsolvedmysteries.com/.

"Is This Hotel Haunted?" *Love Tripper.* Retrieved 7 May 2004.
http://www.lovetripper.com/issues/issue-41/
haunted-historic-inns.html.

"John Stone's Inn (formerly the Ashland Hotel), Ashland, MA." *The Cold
Spot.* Retrieved 4 May 2004. http://www.theflagship.net/coldspot/
docs/hauntedhistory-newengland.html.

Kerrick, Joseph. "Betty Andreasson's Abduction." *The Trigger of Alien
Abduction.* Retrieved 15 June 2004. http://www.near-death.com/
experiences/triggers19.html.

Lagenbach, Randolph. "The Crown and Eagle Mills." *Conservation Tech.*
Retrieved 28 April 2004. http://www.conservationtech.com/
RL's%20resume&%20pub's/RL-publications/Milltowns/1971-
Globe-C&E-MILLS.htm.

Lasalandra, Michael and Merenda, Mark. "Satan's Harvest." *Satan's
Harvest Review.* Retrieved 15 June 2004. http://www.sff.net/people/
doylemacdonald/r_sahar.htm.

"The Legend of Lucy Keyes." *Ghost Stories from around the World.*
Retrieved 18 June 2004. http://www.scaryeyes.com/atw/
displaystory.asp?storyid_566.

"The Legend of Lucy Keyes." *Lucy Keyes.* Retrieved 5 May 2004.
http://www.lucykeyes.com.

"Legends." *Spider Gates.* Retrieved 15 June 2004.
http://spidergates.dcne.net/legends.html.

"Lizzie Borden House." *Ghosts of the World.* Retrieved 26 April 2004.
http://www.hauntedhamilton.com/gotw_lizzieborden.html.

"Lizzie Borden—Information." *Lizzie Borden Bed and Breakfast.* Retrieved
26 April 2004. http://www.lizzie-borden.com/html/information.html.

"Lucy Keyes: A Story of Mt. Wachusett." *New England Magazine and Bay
State Monthly* 4, no. 6 (June 1886): p 551–57.

"Lynn—Lynn Woods Municipal Park: Dungeon Rock." *Ghosts: Boston,
MA and Vicinity.* Retrieved 27 April 2004.
http://www.hollowhill.com/ma/bos.htm.

"MA Case #001—March 1638 or 1639." *Massachusetts Mutual UFO
Network.* Retrieved 11 May 2004. http://www.massmufon.com/
histcas1.html.

"Massachusetts Man Films Six-Foot Metallic Cone-Shaped Object."
Far Shores UFO News. Retrieved 21 June 2004.
http://www.100megsfree4.com/farshores/ufo02ma1.htm.

McGovern, Sharon. "The Legend of Spring Heeled Jack." *The Cobra's
Ghost.* Retrieved 5 May 2004.
http://www.thecobranose.com/xxghosts/shj.html.

"Monster Match: Meet the Warrens." *The Amherst Student Online.*
Retrieved 15 June 2004. http://halogen.note.amherst.edu/
~astudent/2001-2002/issues09/features/01.html.

"The Monster Sea Serpent of Gloucester." *The Unmuseum.* Retrieved
27 April 2004. http://www.unmuseum.org/glserpent.htm.

"Mysterious Sea Serpent Part IV." *Mysterious World.* Retrieved 11 May
2004. http://www.mysteriousworld.com.

"New England's Darkest Day." *Unsolved Mysteries.* Retrieved 30 April
2004. http://www.unsolvedmysteries.com/usm360441.html.

"1909: Cigar-Shaped UFO Follows a Train in Massachusetts." *UFO
Roundup.* Retrieved 5 May 2004.
http://www.parascope.com/nb/uforoundup/uforoundup11.htm.

"1994: Rehoboth's Haunted Cemetery." *UFO Roundup,* vol. 4, no. 27.
Retrieved 28 April 2004. http://www.ufoinfo.com/roundup/v04/
rn27/html.

Nyman, Joseph. "Do UFOs Correct Calendar Watches?" *Massachusetts
MUFON: Cases from the Files.* Retrieved 11 May 2004.
http://www.massmufon.com/case3.html.

"Ogopogo." *True Authority.* Retrieved 1 June 2004.
http://trueauthority.com/cryptozoology/ogopogo.htm.

"Orleans Manufacturing Company." *Historic Sites.* Retrieved 29 June 2004.
http://www.town.rehoboth.ma.us/sites.html.

Bibliography

"Oyster Harbors." Home page. Retrieved 14 July 2004. http://www.falgen.org/Jim/oyster_harbor.htm.

"Petersham." *UFO Sightings Database—UFOs/Aliens.* Retrieved 8 June 2004. http://www.ufos.about.com/library/bldata/bl2mass.htm.

Pittman, Christopher. "The 'Bridgewater Triangle.'" *What Is the Bridgewater Triangle?* Retrieved 21 June 2004. http://www.members.aol.com/soccorro64/btriangle.htm.

———. "A Great Light in the Night." *Massachusetts Case #001.* Retrieved 11 May 2004. http://members.aol.com/soccorro64/1639sighting.htm.

"Pontoosuc Lake." Home page. Retrieved 8 June 2004. http://glenthorne.tripod.com/pontoosuc.html.

"The Reality of a Legend." Home page. Retrieved 27 April 2004. http://www.geocities.com/chrisandjenna441/rrh1.html.

"Restless Spirits?" *Hoosac Tunnel.* Retrieved 8 June 2004. http://www.boudillion.com/hoosac/hoosac.htm.

"The Rockport Witch House Postcard." *Salem Cat.* Retrieved 28 April 2004. http://www.salemcat.com/itm00043.

"Selected Historical Massachusetts Sightings." *Massachusetts Mutual UFO Network.* Retrieved 11 May 2004. http://www.massmufon.com/histcas4.html; http://www.massmufon.com/histcas2.html; http://www.massmufon.com/histcas3.html.

"The Shad Factory Mill and Other Haunts—Nov. 3rd, 2002." Home page. Retrieved 21 June 2004. http://homecast.net/~johnk4678/shad/shad.htm.

"Spider Gates." *New England Paranormal.* Retrieved 5 May 2004. http://www.newenglandparanormal.com.

"Spider Gates Cemetery: The Eighth Gate to Hell?" *Spider Gates.* Retrieved 5 May 2004. http://www.boudillion.com/SpiderGates/spider.html.

Stone, Thomas. "The Hyena Hunt." *Cape Cod Rhymes.* Retrieved 5 May 2004. http://www.capecodhistory.us/books/TNStone-poems.htm.

"Story #1—Dillingham House, Sandwich MA (Spring 1999)." *Cape Cod Ghost Hunters.* Retrieved 19 July 2004. http://www.jpdesign.com/ccgh/stories.htms.

"The Strange Tale of Asa Snow." *Quabbin.* Retrieved 8 June 2004. http://www.westfordcomp.com/quabbin/snow.htm.

"Swallow Cave." *Strange New England.* Retrieved 27 April 2004. http://www.morningstarpublications.com/SwallowCave.html.

Taylor, Troy. "Ghosts of the Bloody Pit." *History and Hauntings of America.* Retrieved 8 June 2004. http://www.prairieghosts.com/hoosac.html.

"Virgin Mary Sightings in the U.S." *Revelation 13.* Retrieved 27 July 2004. http://www.revelation13.net/Mary.html.

Acknowledgments

I'D LIKE TO THANK KYLE WEAVER, MY EDITOR AT STACKPOLE BOOKS, for being in my corner and for his unflappable guidance and support since day one. And many thanks to Amy Cooper and the rest of the talented team at Stackpole for the magic they work. I applaud artist Heather Adel Wiggins for her hauntingly beautiful atmospheric art that blesses these pages.

Many, many thanks to the people who gave me the nod to include various stories in this book, or who otherwise assisted me along the way. They include, but are not limited to, Nicholas Mantello and Charles Blaisdell of the Houghton Mansion, Donald Woods of the Lizzie Borden House, Ed Maas of the Orleans Inn, David Ritchie and Rima Patel of the Omni Parker House Hotel, Sheila FitzGerald and Arpad Voros of the Old Yarmouth Inn, Don Knuuttila of the House of the Seven Gables, Matt Murphy of Stone's Public House, David Grossberg and Jurgen Demisch of the Colonial Inn, Susan Babine of the Hawthorne Hotel, Bob and Marie Scales, John Stimpson, Kay Gill of the Stephen Daniels House, Robert Murphy of the Joshua Ward House, Betty Luca, Jean Durgin, and Ed Richardi of the Barnstable House, and John Pettibone of Hammond House Museum, Inc.

I owe a debt of gratitude to my family and friends, who forgave my occasional absences as I tackled this project. I'm especially grateful to my parents, Tom and Jean Dishaw, and to my siblings, Tom Dishaw, Chris Walker, and Cindy Barry. Their endless support has always been my lifeline. Heartfelt thanks to Judy Farnsworth,

Leland Farnsworth, and Val Deon for their friendship, encourage-ment, and support. Finally, I owe perhaps the most gratitude of all to my husband, Joe, and to our wonderful daughters, Michelle, Jamie, Katie, and Nicole to whom this book is dedicated. Just as sure as the Boston Light never falters, they light up my life and keep my feet firmly planted on solid ground. This one is for them.

About the Author

CHERI REVAI IS THE AUTHOR OF THE BEST-SELLING HAUNTED NORTHERN New York series. She is a native of upstate New York's north country but has many fond memories of family vacations in the adjacent New England states. Her nostalgic recollections, along with a life-long interest in regional history and the paranormal, prompted her to accept the challenge of writing about the strange phenomena of a state she believes may be the most haunted of all—Massachusetts.

Revai lives in northern New York with her family. By day she's a secretary; by night she's an author; and around the clock she's a mother to four daughters. As one of New York's "ghost experts," she has been interviewed extensively by area newspapers and magazines, and has been seen or heard on television and radio broadcasts throughout the Northeast.